BIBLIOTHERAPY

BIBLIOTHERAPY

THE HEALING POWER OF READING

BIJAL SHAH

PIATKUS

PIATKUS

First published in Great Britain in 2024 by Piatkus
This paperback edition published in 2025

SRD

Typeset in Garamond by M Rules
Printed and bound in India by
Manipal Technologies Limited, Manipal

Papers used by Piatkus are from well-managed forests
and other responsible sources.

MIX
Paper | Supporting
responsible forestry
FSC™ C104740

Piatkus
An imprint of
Little, Brown Book Group
Carmelite House
50 Victoria Embankment
London EC4Y 0DZ

An Hachette UK Company
www.hachette.co.uk

www.littlebrown.co.uk

For Amit, Arianna and Roshan, with my love.

Dedicated to readers everywhere.
May this book open new doors of
understanding and healing.

CONTENTS

PART III: THE ART OF LITERARY CURATION

AUTHOR'S NOTE

This is a book for anyone who, like me, has ever turned to literature as a source of comfort, healing, support, understanding and even transformation.

Due to client confidentiality, each story in the book is fictionalised, while being based on true stories and session notes from my bibliotherapy practice. This means that no one client in the book can be identifiable as a real person, and is instead a composite of various case histories. This was necessary to protect client confidentiality and also, sometimes, to clearly illustrate a therapeutic point or psychological truth.

FOREWORD

Of all the things for which we use books – education, entertainment, escapism – one of the more curious is our use of them as a therapeutic medium and a form of social connection. Literature affords us familiar friends through the silent passage of words, as we forge connections with fictional characters who are almost more perfect than the friends we find in real life. This is partly down to the fact that we have uninterrupted access into the minds and emotions of the characters we read, so we experience what feels like a more immediate and sometimes more intense level of intimacy than we would with a close family member or friend. This relationship that evolves between reader and character echoes the celebrity effect, where the familiarity of a favourite celebrity makes us feel that we know them personally. Consider this striking insight offered by Anne Elliot in Jane Austen's *Persuasion*:

> 'The last few hours were certainly very painful,' replied Anne, 'but when pain is over, the remembrance of it often becomes a pleasure. One does not love a place the less for having suffered in it unless it has been all suffering, nothing but suffering.

These words resonate with us. Often the pain of past suffering simply becomes a small footnote in our lives, its significance shed and its power less acute. Austen's observation is so astute that as readers, we find ourselves identifying with and recognising our own experiences in her words. On the other hand, if we've never experienced such pain and suffering, it can feel enlightening to explore these feelings through reading. In sharing in Anne's pain and joy, we feel that we know her intimately. Reading about others' experiences of suffering also offers us a deeper understanding of the extremes of human behaviour – for example, our capacity for extreme cruelty, as we see in Anne Frank's *The Diary of a Young Girl* and Margaret Atwood's *The Handmaid's Tale*. These books allow us to understand another person's experience through empathetic reading, so that we begin to recognise their pain, their suffering, and their experience. In doing so, we can connect with them through the painful emotions they bring up in us, inviting self-exploration and examination, and perhaps even catharsis.

As a bibliotherapist, I've observed that reading affords us a level of intimacy and connection, as well as a sense of being understood, that can be incredibly healing. Books allow us to connect with people with whom we would not otherwise connect in our daily lives, extending our empathetic capabilities, and safely submerging us into a virtual reality that can often feel more 'real' than the one in which we currently reside.

Literature's therapeutic benefits have been known for centuries, but the term 'bibliotherapy' was first coined by American essayist Samuel Crothers in 1916. Crothers believed that reading novels could offer a more affordable and accessible form of therapy, and could, for some patients, even wholly replace psychoanalysis, the pioneering form of therapeutic treatment at the turn of the twentieth century. Widely regarded as the founding father of psychoanalysis, Freud himself was no stranger to the concept of bibliotherapy, and believed that literature could be a useful tool in therapy as it provided a way for clients to explore their own unconscious desires and motivations. In his essay 'Creative Writers and Day-Dreaming'[1] Freud refers to the writer as akin to a therapist who can guide us and help us process our emotions, leading to greater self-awareness and insight.

> The writer of literature creates a world of phantasy which he takes very seriously – that is, which he invests with large amounts of emotion – while separating it sharply from reality ... In my opinion, all the aesthetic pleasure which a creative writer affords us has the character of a fore-pleasure of this kind, and our actual enjoyment of an imaginative work proceeds from a liberation of tensions in our minds ... this effect is due to the writer's enabling us thence forward to enjoy our own day-dreams without self-reproach or shame.

I stumbled upon bibliotherapy while studying psychodynamic counselling, and it was a moment of profound revelation. Literature quickly took centre stage in all my therapy sessions, and this ultimately paved the way to my current bibliotherapy practice and literary curation consultancy. I've noticed remarkable changes in my clients who have engaged with therapeutic reading – whether in their personal or professional lives – and it only seems fitting to share their stories of healing through literature in a book of my own. I want to tell my readers about the bibliotherapy process, and the art of prescribing books that bring meaning, connection and healing.

Using my lived experience both as a bibliotherapee and a bibliotherapist, I will chart bibliotherapy's evolution as a form of therapy by exploring how the concept of therapeutic reading has been developed over the centuries by the ancient Greeks, Michel de Montaigne, William Wordsworth, George Eliot, Freud, hospital librarians during both World Wars and, more recently, academics.

This important history allows us to understand the development of bibliotherapy and its principles. We'll explore my own journey of healing through literature – from growing up in an orthodox Jain* community in Kenya, East Africa, and turning to reading for comfort, to discovering bibliotherapy while training as a counsellor and developing my own bibliotherapy practice – and we'll also look at those of my clients, sharing their stories of healing through literature and offering hope, faith and inspiration to readers everywhere. These accounts cover themes of loss, grief, depression, motherhood, identity, race, gender, neurodiversity and relationship challenges to explore how bibliotherapy has been used as a tool for navigating challenging and complex circumstances.

Our relationship with literature remains our most intimate, because books possess the unique ability to mirror our deepest needs and aspirations. We feel seen, heard and held. Let's leverage this unique ability, using the practice of bibliotherapy to guide, enlighten and eventually transform us.

---

*   Jainism is one of the oldest religions in India. Its premise is that the path to enlightenment is through nonviolence (*ahimsa*) and reducing harm to living things (including plants and animals) as much as possible. Like Hindus and Buddhists, Jains believe in reincarnation. This cycle of birth, death and rebirth is determined by one's karma.

HOW TO USE THIS BOOK

This book is divided into three sections, 'Part I: Bibliotherapy – An Introduction', 'Part II: Bibliotherapy Journeys' and 'Part III: The Art of Literary Curation'.

In Part I, I offer an understanding of bibliotherapy, what it is, how it developed over millennia and how I came to practise it.

In Part II, I explore my relationship with books and how it has shaped who I am today. I also share stories from my therapy room, with each chapter featuring a different client, to illustrate how bibliotherapy can be used to address a range of anxieties and concerns. At the end of each chapter, you will find a tailored reading list that was prescribed as well as the bibliotherapy and complimentary therapeutic techniques used. Exercises that will allow you to practise each of these techniques at home are also included.

In Part III, I share how to create your own curated reading lists and offer an A-Z selection of book prescriptions, which are broken down by theme and can be used as reference points when putting together your own lists. The titles included span fiction, non-fiction and poetry across a variety of genres.

PART I

Bibliotherapy –
An Introduction

1

DISCOVERY OF A NOVEL THERAPY

> 'If the head and body are to be well, you must begin
> by curing the soul; that is the first thing. And the cure,
> my dear youth, has to be effected by the use of certain
> charms, and these charms are fair words.'
>
> CHARMIDES, PLATO

August is my birth month. It's my son's and my grandfather's, too. For me, it's always been a month of magic – not that I am remotely superstitious. It's the month when novel, exciting coincidences, unexpected connections and quite simply some of my happiest moments have manifested. I've always thought of it as a time of divine intervention, and the August of 2007 was no different. I vividly recall an epiphany I had that month that sowed the seeds for the birth of this book.

There are few moments of realisation so striking that they render everything else mundane by comparison – but it's these moments that take you by surprise and make life exciting and full of wonder.

Novelist Virginia Woolf encapsulates this feeling in a review she wrote in 1917, describing 'certain moments which break off from the mass, in which without bidding things come together in a combination of inexplicable significance, to arrest those thoughts which suddenly, to the thinker at least, are almost menacing with meaning'.

When I was training to be a counsellor, one of the prerequisites of my course was that I needed to be in therapy myself. A specific session still looms large in my mind, as it was the first time I opened up about a traumatic childhood experience. I remember sitting by the window in a snug blue armchair in my therapist's small, flowery office. It was a summer's day and, as the sun grazed my skin, I felt warm and comforted. In the relaxed atmosphere, I found myself speaking about being trapped as a young child, and how the fear from that day had continued to haunt me well into my adulthood. Simply revisiting the memory would trigger symptoms that mimicked those of post-traumatic stress disorder: flashbacks, panic attacks, overreactions and the irrational feeling of having no escape. Overwhelmed by emotions that I had no way to process as a child, I turned to books as my sanctuary. Reading allowed me to dodge my pain, and it became my means of detaching from the world around me when things became ugly or difficult.

Earlier that day, before meeting with my therapist, I'd been reading Hanya Yanagihara's *A Little Life*, a novel about love and friendship that is really about the legacy of childhood trauma. The protagonist, Jude, is subjected to abuse from a very young age, and the resulting trauma continues to shadow his every move as an adult. Jude's story resonated with me not because his experience closely mirrored mine (my own moment of terror had been a one-off and drew no similarities to what had happened to Jude) but because like Jude, I still carried the fear and pain of my childhood with me. Time and time again, I would find myself reliving the past in the present. When faced with a vaguely threatening situation, I would snap back to being four years old again, trapped, helpless and terrified. The trauma of that moment would reverberate for years to come, continuing to have an impact on both my body and mind. I became someone who was desperate to please and completely conflict-adverse – the thought of conflict made me uncomfortable. It was easier to give in and be 'nice' in order to maintain the peace, even if this meant silencing my own voice and ignoring my needs.

I had never spoken about that memory to anyone until it played out in front of me – in the pages of *A Little Life*:

He was an optimist. Every month, every week, he chose to open his eyes, to live another day in the world. He did it when he was feeling so awful that sometimes the pain seemed to transport him to another state, one in which everything, even the past that he worked so hard to forget, seemed to fade into a gray watercolour wash. He did it when his memories crowded out all other thoughts, when it took real effort, real concentration, to tether himself to his current life, to keep himself from raging with despair and shame. He did it when he was so exhausted of trying, when being awake and alive demanded such energy that he had to lie in bed thinking of reasons to get up and try again.

Now the memory sat there on the pages, floating. I didn't know what to do with it. All I knew was that I felt very compassionate towards Jude, and in turn towards myself, something I hadn't really experienced before. For the first time, I was seeing myself through new eyes. I wrote everything down in my journal and brought it to my therapist.

'Post-traumatic stress disorder, or PTSD,' she said. 'There's unresolved trauma. It's not surprising the book prompted your memories of childhood trauma. Art, and in this case literature, has an uncanny way of drawing out these memories. The book feels like a safe place from which to carry out your own self-examinations at a distance, as it allows you to develop a better understanding of your own character by exploring the experiences of others. After all, everything that we process is really filtered through our own lens of experience.'

She paused, waiting for me to respond.

I stayed silent. I wanted to know more. Learn more.

She continued. 'Have you heard of the case of Epizelus?'

'No,' I responded, curious. 'But I'd love to hear about it.'

Epizelus, she explained, was an Athenian soldier who fought bravely in the Battle of Marathon. Strangely, despite not having been dealt a single blow in battle, he was reported to have suddenly lost his sight. Epizelus never regained his vision and when asked how he came to be blinded, he recalled that 'a gigantic warrior, with a huge beard, which shaded all his shield, stood over against him; but the ghostly semblance passed him by, and slew the man at his side'.[2] He had imagined the phantom passing through his body, and this had resulted in the loss of his sight.

Whether in a contemporary novel or the account of an ancient Greek soldier, I found myself empathising with the protagonists' experiences of PTSD. Or perhaps it was the other way around – the protagonists were empathising with me and validating my own experience as a story to be examined and resolved. This is one of the many super-powers of literature: the ability to empathise and to be empathised with. In his book *Our Better Angels*, psychologist and bestselling author Steven Pinker explains that society as a whole experienced an increased capacity for empathy during the Enlightenment and, in some ways, this correlates with the rise of the novel, especially British epistolary novels such as Samuel Richardson's *Clarissa* and *Pamela*. The epistolary novel takes the form of a series of letters, diary entries or other written correspondences between characters, enabling multiple perspectives, realism and intimacy. It allows unique access to the characters' innermost thoughts and feelings. We might feel more connected to the protagonist or narrator on an emotional level, giving us a better understanding of their motivations, fears and desires. The conversational style feels more authentic and realistic, while the multiple perspectives allow us to see the story or events from different points of view, giving us a stronger picture of the overarching narrative and the interpersonal relationships of the characters. This further deepens our emotional investment in the story, increasing our ability to empathise with the characters and immerse ourselves in their experiences.

Reflecting on this idea, I was reminded of two novels, although not epistolary, that I felt particularly drawn to. The first was George Eliot's *Mill on the Floss* which I had read as a teenager and the deep connection I'd felt to its heroine, Maggie, who constantly sought approval from a stern older brother. Secondly, my thoughts also turned to Konstantin Levin in Leo Tolstoy's *Anna Karenina*, a character who ruminated intensely over what makes life worth living. I felt incredibly soothed and comforted after reading the tragic yet profoundly human stories of these characters. It was as though I was validating and healing my own wounds by connecting to their experiences, relieving me of my pain and kickstarting the recovery process. It felt liberating.

While thinking about these three novels, I realised that literature had provided an outlet for me to address darker, knottier emotions that I had shied away from in my own reality. Was this because I felt in control when reading? I could choose when I wanted to put down my book, and perhaps this provided a sense of security. The more I considered it, the more the process of reading began to resemble the elements present in a therapy room: a relationship with someone with whom you felt safe to explore your innermost thoughts and feelings, and the agency to walk away if it all felt too much. It dawned on me: was the literary relationship between text and reader a therapeutic one?

As I processed this, I was compelled to find out more about literature as a therapeutic medium, so as soon as I got home from my session, I googled 'literature as therapy'. I came across a definition in a piece by Debbie McCulliss in the *Journal of Poetry Therapy* titled 'Bibliotherapy: Historical and Research Perspectives',[3] and immediately clicked on it.

Bibliotherapy is derived from a combination of two Greek words, *biblion* (meaning book) and *therapeia* (meaning healing). The term bibliotherapy was coined in 1916 by Samuel McChord Crothers (1916), a Unitarian minister and essayist. Initially, the term was used to describe literature used in counselling people suffering from mental illness. The earliest formal definition of bibliotherapy appeared in the 11th edition of *Dorland's Illustrated Medical Dictionary* in 1941. In 1961, *Webster's Third New International Dictionary*'s definition of bibliotherapy was accepted by the American Library Association (ALA): 'the use of selected reading materials as therapeutic adjuncts in medicine and psychiatry; also, guidance in the solution of personal problems through directed reading'.

Intrigued and transfixed, I went down a rabbit hole of web searches. Therapeutic literature was often viewed as a supportive or adjunct psychotherapy. As a book lover, this was music to my ears. I wanted to go deeper still, to a wonderland where the whole emotional richness of the literary world could take hold. Reading had always felt cathartic for me, but now I had a name for its ability to help process my emotions: *bibliotherapy*. The word rolled delightfully off my tongue. For the next few days, I read research papers and articles, explored studies that tested the hypothesis of literature as a therapeutic medium, and delved into the practice's rich history. I knew I had landed on something remarkable, and I had a sudden and impatient desire to share this with others who could also benefit from it and thrive thanks to the healing power of reading.

A SHORT HISTORY OF BIBLIOTHERAPY

This section details the evolution of bibliotherapy and chronologically explores the work of both early and modern-day pioneers of bibliotherapy.

Some of the ideas and history I outline were inspired by the research of Dr Kelda Green, whom I interviewed for an article in 2020. Dr Green's research, as part of her doctoral thesis at the Centre for Research into Reading, Literature and Society at the University of Liverpool, focused on rethinking therapeutic reading.[4] Here I synthesise some of her ideas and include my own sources and supporting research.

The Ancient Greeks

Book therapy or bibliotherapy can be traced back to the ancient Greeks, who built libraries not dissimilar to the libraries of today. Their influence on language, politics, education, philosophy, science, literature and the arts can still be felt to this day, which is a testament to their dedication and commitment to learning. In fact, the Greeks played a pioneering role in the development of a number of literary genres, including poetry, theatre and the novel,* all of which form the foundations of therapeutic literature. For example, the great philosopher Aristotle argued that tragedy was a form of art that aimed to evoke emotions in its audience through plot, character and language, ultimately providing catharsis.† He also promoted the importance of self-reflection and self-knowledge,[5] two qualities that are integral parts of therapeutic reading, which requires observation of our thoughts and emotions, and self-reflection and processing of these to arrive at understanding and healing.

Seneca and the Stoics emerged a century after Aristotle.

---

*   The earliest novels include ancient Greek and Latin ones from the first century BC to the second century AD, such as Chariton's *Callirhoe* as well as Heliodorus' *An Ethiopian Story* and Lucian's *A True Story*, according to B. P. Reardon's *Collected Ancient Greek Novels*.

†   See chapter 6 of Aristotle's *Poetics* as translated by S. H. Butcher: 'Tragedy, then, is an imitation of an action that is serious, complete, and, of a certain magnitude; in language embellished with each kind of artistic ornament, the several kinds being found in separate parts of the play; in the form of action, not of narrative, through pity and fear effecting the proper purgation of these emotions.'

Stoicism is an ancient Greek and Roman school of philosophy that was developed in the early third century BC, and evolved as a way to navigate life's uncertainty and the inevitability of misfortune and suffering. Our understanding and knowledge of Stoicism comes largely from the writings of three giants: Seneca, Epictetus and Marcus Aurelius.

Stoics believed that it was important to live virtuously, and to embrace what is in our control and to surrender to what is not. Stoicism is founded on the principles of logic, reason and ethics. Through self-control, integrity and strength of mind, we can begin to think clearly and in unbiased ways so that we can gain freedom from negative emotions such as anger, envy and jealousy, no matter how difficult our circumstances. The judgement and opinions we assign to thoughts are what can trigger these negative emotions, leading to suffering (*pathos*). As Epictetus wrote, 'Men are not disturbed by things, but by their opinions of them.'

This approach has been adopted in modern talking therapies, specifically forming the basis of cognitive behavioural therapy (CBT). CBT is a talking therapy pioneered by psychologist Albert Ellis and psychiatrist Aaron T. Beck. It looks at the influence our thoughts can have on our feelings and physical sensations. Beck and Ellis have described how they used Stoicism to develop the ABC model for emotions that forms the basis of CBT as author Jules Evans describes in his book, *Philosophy for Life*: 'We experience an event (A); then interpret it (B), and then feel an emotional response in line with our interpretation (C). Ellis, following the Stoics, suggested that we can change our emotions by changing our thoughts or opinions about events.'

Stoicism permeates much of Western thought and literature, and its teachings can offer great comfort, healing and insight.

Michel de Montaigne

Sixteenth-century French writer and philosopher Michel de Montaigne was another giant of therapeutic literature. Montaigne was known for writing essays that offered honest and astute observations about his life, and his introspection and examination of what it meant to be alive invited readers to consider their own circumstances and perspectives.[6] He wrote 107 essays exploring questions relating to the human condition, from dealing with the loss of a loved one to accepting human fallibility, but he also explored more mundane, day-to-day dilemmas, such as how to avoid useless quarrels with loved ones, how to lift someone's spirits, and the art of the polite exit. His style of writing, which tended to be more intimate[*] and conversational than the typical essay, came to be known as 'the personal essay', and he was one of the pioneers of the form.[†] For Montaigne, the personal essay was a medium for self-examination that used writing as a tool to work through difficult issues and achieve understanding.

Today, we see this process in practice in memoirs and personal essay collections, which have become portals for permissible self-exploration and observation. Works such as these offer libraries of information on selfhood: who are we, how should we be, how should we live, what's meaningful to us? The multiple perspectives and mysteries of life are found here. The memoirist or narrator begins

---

[*]   'The hallmark of the personal essay is its intimacy. The writer seems to be speaking directly into your ear, confiding everything from gossip to wisdom,' states Phillip Lopate in his book *The Art of the Personal Essay*.

[†]   Refer to *The Origins of the Essay* by John D'Agata (Graywolf Press, 2009) and *Montaigne's English Journey: Reading the Essays in Shakespeare's Day* by William M. Hamlin (Oxford University Press, 2014).

with a personal issue or crisis at the heart of the self that is usually linked to conflict or suffering. As they work through their feelings and thoughts, we are eventually led to catharsis, revelation and transformation.

Montaigne's exploration of universal themes, written with openness, honesty and authenticity, allows his work to resonate with readers today and keeps the therapeutic magic of his writing alive.

Wordsworth

Wordsworth, 'the healing poet', also drew comfort from the Stoics, capturing Stoic wisdom* as well as a Montaigne-like exploration of the self.

Wordsworth's poetry gives life to pain and loss by converting it into something valuable and meaningful – a quiet resilience, giving us hope even in the midst of suffering – and enabling us to connect our pain with something like beauty. It reminds me of the Japanese philosophy of *wabi sabi*, which embraces the beauty in the transience and imperfection of all things. There's beauty in the broken, value in loss and suffering. In a similar vein, Wordsworth's poetry fills us with hope and healing, pointing us towards growth and an aliveness that's often absent from Stoicism. His work was part of larger cultural movement taking shape during the Romantic era at the end of the eighteenth century and the beginning of the nineteenth. Inspired by the French Revolution, there was significant social change during this time, and an emphasis on individuals and emotion over reason. Emotion had begun to receive particular emphasis and is found in

---

* In her book *Wordsworth's Reading of Roman Prose*, Jane Worthington discusses the influence of Stoicism on Wordsworth and his poetry.

most poetry of the era, with a focus on individual thought and personal feeling.

George Eliot

George Eliot's novels are recognised for their psychological depth and complexity, and her contribution to psychological realism in literature remains notable. She was filling a space previously held by religion with the more scientific concepts of early psychology, as is evident in the way her novels offer comfort, hope, and a space for reflection and empathy. She gave readers a language through which to express the emotions that resulted from the bittersweet complexity of human existence, allowing us to appreciate and accept conflict and ambivalence as the realities of daily life.

Eliot's novel *Daniel Deronda*, written prior to the publication of Freud's initial theories on psychoanalysis, is almost the precursor to Freud's thinking on the healing power of human relationships.[7] Some of the aspects of a therapeutic relationship we see in Freud's theories seem to stem from Eliot's writings: offering an intimate ear, suspending judgement and moral criticism, offering a space to hold opposing contradictions together, showing empathy, acknowledging the role of the unconscious, and considering the significance of transference.

In *Daniel Deronda*, Eliot also focuses on the characters' childhoods to illustrate the conflicts that drive their behaviour, noting that Daniel's identity issues are due to being painfully abandoned by his mother in early childhood, while Gwendolen's ambivalence towards men is due to the loss of her father when she was young. All these insights were before Freud's time, yet seem to echo the basis of psychoanalytical theory: that our childhood relationships influence all our future relationships, and we often attract similar relationships to the ones we experienced in our childhood.

Freud's admiration for Eliot's work is reflected in his gift-giving; he was always offering Eliot's novels as gifts to friends and family. He even mentions Eliot's *Adam Bede* in his book *The Interpretation of Dreams*.[8] Eliot's writing captured the ways in which feelings and emotions are revealed in subtle ways, highlighting her astute observations of non-verbal expression. She was a master of writing about relationships, especially therapeutic ones, and recognising that we are not all bad or all good, but simply vulnerable, psychologically flawed beings with conflicts.

Freud

Freud was also influenced by the ancient Greek tragedies, and he drew on many Stoic texts and ideas in the development of his psychoanalytic theories.* In particular, he was interested in the works of Greek tragedians like Sophocles and Euripides, as well as the writings of philosophers like Plato and Aristotle. As discussed in his books *The Interpretation of Dreams*[9] and *Introductory Lectures on Psychoanalysis*,[10] one of Freud's key contributions to psychoanalysis was his concept of the Oedipus complex, named after the character King Oedipus in Sophocles' play *Oedipus Rex*. Freud saw this play as a powerful exploration of the human psyche and the unconscious mind, and he used it to develop his theories about the ways in which unconscious desires and impulses can shape human behaviour.

---

* In *Freud: The Mind of the Moralist,* Philip Reid highlights the relationship between psychoanalysis and the psychological theories of Stoicism.

In addition to the Oedipus complex, Freud also drew on a wide range of other Greek sources in his work, including ideas about the importance of dreams and the role of the unconscious mind in shaping human behaviour. He saw Greek culture and philosophy as a rich source of insights into the human psyche, and he believed that these insights could be used to develop more effective approaches to psychotherapy. For example, Freud first introduces his application of the myth of Oedipus from Greek mythology to explain the concept of the Oedipus complex. He saw Oedipus as a symbolic representation of a child's emotional conflict between desire and hostility towards their parents. He introduces this idea in his seminal work *The Interpretation of Dreams* in 1899.

In his essay 'Creative Writers and Day-dreaming'[11] Freud refers to the writer as someone who enables us to enjoy our own fantasies (daydreams) without shame or self-reproach, suggesting that reading allows us to explore our innermost thoughts, desires and conflicts by offering a safe space to release repressed tensions without risking unpleasant consequences. Freud's emphasis on open and honest self-examination draws similarities with Montaigne's approach to writing about the self. Author Adam Phillips observes in the *Penguin Freud Reader* that there is 'a contagious energy about Freud's writing', noting that 'for some people, Freud's writing was the kind of reading experience that was (and is) more akin to a conversion experience ... Freud's sentences had what might be called a religious effect on people'.

Early Nineteenth Century

In the early nineteenth century, on the other side of the Atlantic, physicians and authors Benjamin Rush and John Galt were pioneering the use of bibliotherapy in their own practices under the umbrella term 'moral therapy', which included activities like gardening, woodworking, sewing and reading.[12] It was within this moral therapy movement that bibliotherapy gained traction,[13] with both Rush and Galt prescribing reading as a therapeutic tool to their patients.

Galt wrote: 'To many patients, [reading] proves a source of agreeable feelings during time which would otherwise be full of the tedium of ennui.'[14] He also stressed the importance of libraries, advocating for their presence in the many asylums being established at that time.[15]

Early Twentieth Century

Libraries were an important component of European psychiatric institutions enabling the practice of bibliotherapy. At the turn of the twentieth century, bibliotherapy began to gain traction as a practice both in the UK and across the Atlantic, with books and explorations of bibliotherapy widely available in hospitals.

If the library movement had a poster child, it was Edith Kathleen Jones. Her 1913 book *A Thousand Books for the Hospital Library* was written:

> as a guide towards the selection of wholesome, readable literature
> for those who are ill either physically or mentally. While it has
> been compiled with the requirements of the latter class of patients
> in mind, it would seem no less suitable for the former, or, in fact,
> for any small library which desires only bright, wholesome, inter-
> esting books.[16]

At this time, hospital librarianship was emerging as a relatively new field, and Jones was one of the few hospital librarians with sufficient experience to write a book on the topic and pull together helpful reading lists for patients. The American Library Association (ALA) endorsed bibliotherapy as a form of medical treatment in their 1938 *National Plan for Libraries*.[17] In 1939, the ALA published another book by Jones, *Hospital Libraries*, which addressed current and best practices in therapeutic reading. Historian and writer Monique S. Dufour states that 'the book was heralded as a pivotal achievement for the profession in a time of optimism and successes'.[18]

Sadie Peterson Delaney, pioneer bibliotherapist and chief librarian at the Veterans Administration Hospital in Tuskegee, Alabama, also extensively used bibliotherapy in her work at this time, selecting reading material with which to treat patients and readers.[19]

The practice gained further recognition in the 1950s when Caroline Shrodes, an American academic and author of *The Conscious Reader*, theorised that characters in stories can be hugely influential to readers who identify with them, suggesting that the interaction of personality and imaginative literature can help release emotions into the conscious realm, where we can draw value from them, whether that is through obtaining a sense of self-awareness, gaining relief from painful feelings or finding a form of closure.

Shrodes's theory and research outline an important and practical framework that draws parallels with more traditional psychodynamic counselling training, which I'll explore further in the next chapter. She refers to Freud's impact on therapeutic reading in her essay 'Bibliotherapy: An Application of Psychoanalytic Theory',[20] in which she compares the relationship between reader and text to Freud's therapist–client relationship, noting the shared psychological reality that fiction can provide between the reader and the character through identification, connection and catharsis. Shrodes states: 'It is a process of interaction between the personality of the reader and imaginative literature which may engage his emotions and free them for conscious and productive use.'

She notes the reader must feel safe to explore feelings provoked by the text, relaxing their defences and being willing to explore the value of literary thinking and find meaning within the language through self-reflection, journaling and/or discussion with a therapist. The reading and reflection process should enable self-awareness, with a sense of freedom and agency emerging.

Late Twentieth Century and Early Twenty-First

More recently, researchers have also studied the cognitive impact of reading on people's minds and found remarkable results. In 1983, husband and wife team Gordan Sabine and Patricia Sabine, professors of journalism at Virginia Tech and Ohio State University respectively, interviewed 1,382 avid readers around the United States as part of the 'Books That Made the Difference' project.[21] The participants chosen represented a diverse demographic, including some celebrities as well as everyday readers across a variety of ages, professions and locations.

The focus of the survey was gathering information on what books made the greatest difference in the readers' lives, and what that difference was. Based on the interviews, readers reported the impact books had made on them, such as inspiring them to overcome challenges, changing their mindsets, reinforcing new ways of thinking, helping them pursue a new career, or even serving as escapism to 'get away from it all'. Most of all, sixty per cent of readers reported that reading was personally transformative. One reader, a young man in his twenties, reported that he had been contemplating suicide after planning to split up from his wife, but after reading the book *Life After Life* by Raymond A. Moody, about 'people who have survived bodily death, and people who believe the soul lives on after death', he was transformed – he wanted to live. Another man found *The Keys of the Kingdom*, a book detailing the life story of a lovable Scottish priest, to be deeply comforting while grieving the death of his mother. A third found *The Big Book* of Alcoholics Anonymous instrumental in treating his alcoholism.

In 2009, researchers at the University of Toronto undertook a study testing the hypothesis that 'art can cause significant changes in the experience of one's personality traits'.[22] In the study, participants either read Chekov's 'The Lady with the Toy Dog' or a control text (the same story written in factual, documentary style, of the same length and complexity but lacking the aesthetic quality of Chekhov's work), and completed a before-and-after questionnaire of The Big Five Inventory (a personality trait questionnaire that assesses the 'big five' traits: conscientiousness, agreeableness, openness, extraversion and emotional stability), as well as an emotional checklist assessing ten emotions (happiness, sadness, anxiety, boredom, unsettledness, anger, fearfulness, contentment, excitement, awe). None of the participants had read the short story before. Participants who read Chekhov's short story experienced notably greater changes in personality than the control group and relayed being more emotionally moved, confirming that their change in personality was a result of the emotions evoked by the text. The researchers concluded that personality shifts brought on by reading fiction are worth exploring.

THE ROLE OF WRITING IN BIBLIOTHERAPY

The best writers tend to write what they know, and often their writing can be semi-autobiographical, inspired by personal experiences, so as part of the creative process they need to work through their own emotions. Their writing can be cathartic, and this *emotional experience* is passed on to readers, enabling readers to connect with the writing in a more profound and meaningful way while also being healed by it.

Inspired, I began to journal every time I read. I refer to this process as literary journaling, and it involves thinking deeply about what I've read, observing my emotional reactions, considering what the writing was bringing up for me, and acknowledging what I'd learned about myself through the process. Mindfully reading, page by page, I was creating my own parallel narrative, shaping the heroine of my own story, as Joseph Campbell, author of *The Hero with a Thousand Faces*, would say. The journaling enabled self-compassion and connection to both the text and myself – all key ingredients for healing. Journaling has now become a key part of my practice, as you'll see in the coming chapters.

EMBRACING TRANSFORMATION THROUGH BIBLIOTHERAPY

My interest in bibliotherapy encouraged me to take stock, and I completed an audit of sorts by reviewing how books had changed me over the years. They had been a constant source of support throughout my life. I remembered my parents sending me to England as a seven-year-old to spend eight weeks of summer with extended family and the excitement and nervousness that followed. To put myself at ease, I thought about Roald Dahl's *Matilda*, *The BFG* and *James and the Giant Peach*, all of which featured protagonists who had to fend for themselves without the loving support of a parent. I thought that if Matilda, Sophie and James could go it alone in much more challenging conditions, then I could stick it out for at least a couple of months without my parents.

My mind then turned to memories of a painful break-up that I'd experienced when I was twenty-four, and how Nicole Krauss's *A History of Love* rescued me. It was my first break-up and the overwhelming feelings of sadness and longing were simply too painful for me to process so I shut down emotionally instead. It wasn't until reading *A History of Love* that I allowed the tears that I'd been holding back to flow freely. Immediately I felt understood and less alone, and this experience reiterated to me the remarkable power of words to navigate love and loss. I documented these experiences, journaling alongside, to capture the micro-transformations that had occurred over time.

My new bibliotherapy journaling practice helped me notice small changes within myself. I took these reflections to my therapist, who reinforced these positive changes by offering moral support. The whole process worked hand in hand, reinventing me – book by book, session by session.

Poetry Therapy

While novels and non-fiction played a significant role in my healing, poetry did too. I had experienced friendship break-ups and losses that felt devastating. Relationships that felt solid and lifelong had actually turned out to be fragile and temporary. This realisation offered clarity, but the sense of loss felt overwhelming and monstrous. I was enveloped in a shroud of sadness and anger, and I no longer had the energy to contain either. Poetry helped me to make sense of what was happening. It succinctly captures our charged emotions, and it's in the midst of these emotions that some of the best poems are written. As the words cathartically appear on paper, we begin to heal. The therapy happens in the writing.

Poetry's powerful healing qualities have been documented during both World Wars and the American Civil War; poems were read to soldiers to help them cope with trauma and the brutalities of conflict. Doctors would write poems for their patients, emotionally connecting with them. A striking example of this is John Keats, who trained as a doctor. Today, poetry is prescribed by modern-day doctors and physicians at Yale University School of Medicine and University College London School of Medicine, while Yale maintains a required literary reading list that includes poetry.

The use of poetry continues to grow as a recognised form of therapy. More and more psychotherapists across the US, UK and Europe are using poetry therapy as part of their practice. Globally, the International Federation for Biblio/Poetry Therapy sets standards of excellence in the training and credentialling of practitioners in the field of poetry therapy, qualifying them to practise.

Below is the first draft of a poem I penned. It's not about the style; it's about poetry's importance as an outlet through which to channel our emotions.

Transitions

A journey's death births another.
A reincarnation.
A natural pause to take stock and reflect.
To better unhelpful habits.
To hit reset.
To rein in life's challenges.

To realign to the bigger vision.
Redesign.
To smile in the face of memories.
To celebrate.
To cry for good times gone.
For special times that inevitably ended.

For time that no longer is.
To mourn loss.
Each journey breaking the groundhog routine of life.
Forcing us to reiterate, pivot and optimise.
Quietly demanding that we re-evaluate
To learn valuable lessons.

Permit celebration.
Merge excitement and hope.
Making sense of life.
Building character.
Diversifying life experience.
Making us whole.

It's not one long road.
It's zig-zags.
Surprising turning points that compound.
Building momentum, as it gives shape to a gigantic, long game.
That in hindsight is absolutely perfect.

It's ultimately our story.

I read poems on friendships as well as writing them. They brought hope, helping me to appreciate the exquisite and blessed relationships I did have in my life. They served as antidotes to the challenging boundary work I was doing. In Gillian Jones's poem 'A Friend', there was the gentle reminder that to have good friends, we need to *be* great friends, too, while Robert Frost's 'A Time to Talk' highlights the importance of making time for friends, and William's Blake's 'A Poison True' explores the danger of bottling up our feelings about friends. As I connected with poets and poems, I often experienced a piece as though it had been written for me specifically. The wisdom of the poems carried me through.

A DEFINITION OF BIBLIOTHERAPY

As my personal literary exploration drew to a close, my own definition of bibliotherapy emerged:

An art therapy that leverages the power of stories to heal. Its magic lies in the relationship formed between the reader and the writing, fiction or non-fiction, poetry or essay, and the reflection of the thoughts, feelings, observations and lessons that the writing provokes, through a daily journaling practice ('literary journaling') or counselling.

Journaling and various bibliotherapy techniques became my toolkit. It was almost a new form of emotional literacy – I would read, reflect, analyse, discuss, process. Therapy has always been a complex undertaking; this was no different. I felt ready, all set to share my insights and techniques with others, to help them find solace and healing in literature, and to help them process buried emotions that felt too painful to dig (and once dug, too painful to feel).

Through literature, you never hold your feelings directly. You observe them in others. Someone else carries your pain. While this is a reflection of yourself, you are held by the literature, empathised with. The safety of someone else feeling and carrying your own difficult emotions while you address and come to terms with them is transformative. Plus, reading about other people's negative emotions makes it easier for us to accept the same negative feelings in ourselves. For only by feeling pain, can we be liberated from it – the basis for catharsis.

With this epiphany, I began to welcome clients into my space, inviting them to bring their pain, their loss and grief, their stresses and anxieties, their traumas, their relationship issues, their identity, gender and sexuality struggles, and their learning disability challenges, such as dyslexia, so that they too, from a distance, yet so intimately entwined with the text, could feel seen, carried, held and empathised with.

And eventually healed.

2

BIBLIOTHERAPY – WHAT IT IS, AND HOW AND WHY IT WORKS

'Art is the nearest thing to life; it is a mode of amplifying experience and extending our contact with our fellowmen beyond the bounds of our personal lot.'

GEORGE ELIOT, *THE NATURAL HISTORY OF GERMAN LIFE.*

WHAT IS BIBLIOTHERAPY?

If what we think of as traditional therapy is often referred to as the 'talking cure', then bibliotherapy is what I call the 'reading cure'. It brings with it an added dimension to healing by providing almost immediate access to the unconscious mind through the realm of the imagination. Not only are the words on the page 'talking to us', but they also take us on a magical journey into the depths of our unconscious, where we visit the recesses of our minds that we've kept neglected for years, or encounter spaces and desires that we never even knew existed.

Freud's free association method (freely sharing thoughts, words and anything else that comes to mind) in talk therapy is automatically enabled in bibliotherapy; literature triggers our minds to unearth and reconnect with forgotten memories through the characters and the situations in which they find themselves, and/or the author's writing ('the vicarious experience'), without the need for an external therapist. Of course, you have the choice to discuss the thoughts and feelings that emerge with a bibliotherapist, counsellor, psychotherapist or similar if you prefer. Alternatively, creative bibliotherapy methods, such as journaling, letter-writing or creative writing, allow us to process the observations, reflections or feelings that arise. By their very nature, these *active* bibliotherapy processes can be more effective than talking therapy as they allow us to freely express and process our feelings and innermost thoughts, without the risk of another's judgement.

HOW DOES BIBLIOTHERAPY WORK?

One of the most important pioneers of bibliotherapy, academic Dr Caroline Shrodes, wrote that 'bibliotherapy is made possible by the "shock of recognition" the reader experiences when he beholds himself, or those close to him, in a story or some other piece of literature'.[23] She believed the author creates an alternative reality, a simulation, that appears so lifelike that the reader's emotions are channelled within this reality, creating an opportunity for both observation and reflection that might offer new perspectives, understanding and insight. Shrodes viewed reading as being much like any other form of living – for example, working, socialising, indulging, educating – and felt that we read entirely with our needs, goals, defences and values in mind.

Echoing traditional psychotherapy, Shrodes felt that for a literary text to qualify as a conduit for healing, three qualities needed to be satisfied: identification (including projection and introjection), catharsis and insight.

- **Identification:** The reader identifies with and connects with the text or relevant character.
- **Catharsis:** The text enables the reader to connect with their own emotions and release these (allowing for a 'cathartic response').
- **Insight:** The text provides insight into the reader's own situation based on the issues faced by the character, and allows the individual to consolidate this insight and learning in a therapeutic fashion.

The idea is that the reader will embrace the connection, empathy or validation that may be triggered within them, and reject the writing or passages that feel too threatening or challenge the ego. Most importantly, like any other form of therapy, the goal is for repetitive patterns of thinking that are no longer serving us to be broken down, and instead for new ways of looking at the world to be encouraged. These shifts in perspective help us to work out what is our personal baggage and what we're holding on to for someone else.

HOW TRANSFERENCE WORKS IN
BIBLIOTHERAPY

In traditional therapy, transference enables the client to see the link between earlier repressed feelings and their later recurrence in the therapist–client relationship. The new perspective or insight they acquire frees them from these repressed emotions.

In bibliotherapy, transference occurs when a reader identifies with a character in a book or a certain situation presented in a story that triggers an emotional response. These emotions are projected on to the author or character, making possible a new experience of the old, unsettled conflict through literature. As we become aware of these feelings, we can process them through journaling, the bibliotherapy techniques I'll share in this book, or counselling and psychotherapy, and in doing so, we can come away with a new perspective. The reading process here acts as a catalyst for freeing these repressed emotions from the unconscious mind.

I remember a particular session with Lucy, a client who felt enraged when reading about Daisy Buchanan, a socialite and one of the central characters in F. Scott Fitzgerald's *The Great Gatsby*. As we explored the feelings triggered by her reading experience, Lucy realised that she was projecting the hostility she felt towards her mother on to Daisy. A deeper interrogation of her reaction to *The Great Gatsby* allowed Lucy to understand that her mother was not perfect, and while she resented her mother's obsession with wealth and status, she could also appreciate her dedication to her children. Growing up, Lucy's mother had always ensured that Lucy and her brother had everything they needed, and she had remained a constant in their lives – unlike Daisy, whom Fitzgerald depicts as having very little interest in her infant daughter. Although it took some time to unpick and address her relationship with her mother, Lucy's realisation allowed her to see her mother from a new perspective and to accept her for who she was – the good parts and the less good ones. In doing so, Lucy was liberated from the ambivalent feelings she had held towards her mother.

Lucy's story demonstrates how bibliotherapy presents us with clues to consider: why do we feel fear, anger, or guilt? Is there something in our past or present that's causing us to project these feelings on to the page? Is it something that we need to address? All of these emotions need to be explored further rather than ignored or rejected. To be able to sit with uncomfortable emotions and process them, no matter how painful they are, is half the work in both therapy and bibliotherapy. Only then can life-changing self-awareness, and a sense of freedom and agency, emerge.

Psychiatrist and academic Professor Murray Bowen said: 'It is better to make allies of, than enemies of, one's emotions. To rid oneself of troublesome projections, one must become aware of them.'[24] In essence, in order to truly find emotional freedom, we must allow ourselves to experience our emotions fully, rather than burying or rejecting them. And literatures gives us the opportunity to do just this: to express our emotions through our reading experience, rather than repressing or withholding them. We begin to unpick and unpack, to process and un-process, to embrace or to reject; at each point, the writing is telling us something if we choose to pay attention, to observe and reflect. Exploring these clues is how patterns of the past shift.

BIBLIOTHERAPY VS OTHER THERAPIES

Bibliotherapy is unique in comparison to other therapies because it has a dual dynamic: it affords the reader the ability to be a bystander and a partaker at the same time; to embrace fantasy and yet find meaning in our reality. By confronting and understanding the perspective of a character or an author, we might begin to recognise their turmoil or happiness in ourselves. Secondary characters may remind us of people in our own lives whom we haven't previously appreciated or understood, and exploring their motivations through literature might be refreshingly comforting and enable you to tolerate their imperfections in a more balanced way, or perhaps lessen your fear of or ambivalence towards them.

Sometimes, experiencing a new emotion that we recognise intuitively through a character's experience, but have yet to put into words, can unearth older emotions attached to a difficult memory or conflicting experience, inviting a new perspective – and possibly resolution.

Academics Dr Geoff Kaufman and Dr Lisa Libby have found that 'losing yourself' in the world of a fictional character when reading can lead to an actual change in your own behaviour.[25] In a study carried out at Ohio State University, Kaufman and Libby observed that readers would engage in 'experience-taking', defined as 'the imaginative process of spontaneously assuming the identity of a character in a narrative and simulating that character's thoughts, emotions, behaviours, goals, and traits as if they were one's own'. This shift can lead to very real – permanent or temporary – changes. An example of it in practice was evidenced when participants in the study who identified strongly with a fictional character who had overcome obstacles to vote were shown to be significantly more likely to go out and vote in a real election a few days later. Participants who read about characters who they later discovered were of a different race or sexual orientation were more likely to react positively towards the character as well as anyone whom they encountered in person who was of a similar race or sexual orientation, embracing and stereotyping them less through the process of 'experience-taking'. For it to truly work, the reader is required to completely lose themselves in the character in order to temporarily take on the character's identity and worldview. The study also found that a first-person narrative was far more powerful in causing this shift to experience-taking than a third-person one, as was delaying the revelation of the character's gender, race, class and sexual identity and orientation.

Benefits of Bibliotherapy as a Therapeutic Practice

- Increased self-awareness. By reading about characters and situations in books, individuals can gain new insights into their own emotions and behaviours. We see with clarity where protagonists fail, and this can help to shed light on our own blind spots.
- Reading ignites our imaginations, clarifies our emotions and honours our own very human problems. It also offers respite, or solutions to these problems, as well as offering a sense of meaning, enriching us.

- Reading, like meditation, produces changes in the brain that increase executive function and better regulation of emotions, so that you are better able to select the relevant emotion for a given situation, reducing symptoms of stress, anxiety and depression.
- Like reading, writing also heals us, and creative bibliotherapy techniques (a mixture of reading and writing practices) allow us to begin consciously and unconsciously processing our emotions, enabling healing.

THE THREE PILLARS OF BIBLIOTHERAPY

As I mentioned earlier, Caroline Shrodes's theory and research outlines an important and practical framework that draws parallels with traditional psychodynamic counselling and therapy: for a literary text to heal, the qualities of (i) identification (ii) catharsis and (iii) insight and/or action must be met. Underpinning these pillars is a sense of safety, trust and connection.

Safety and Trust

As in conventional therapy, for any therapeutic process to take place, a client must feel safe. The therapeutic process takes place between your eye and the page of a book in a safe, physical space that could be at home, or in the therapy room if you're working with a bibliotherapist or similar mental health professional. The point is, wherever you are engaging in bibliotherapy, you must feel a sense of safety, security and trust. The reader must trust the writing and feel safe to explore the feelings and observations that it provokes. These can be explored by either journaling or discussing any feelings that arise with a close friend or in therapy (either group or individual). Studies have shown that talking about a character's issues rather than our own feels safer, due to the distance it creates – we can explore the issues without the fear of judgement we might feel exposed to when expressing how we feel to another person, even a counsellor or therapist.

In my experience, even the most defensive of clients, those who are more resistant towards conventional forms of counselling and therapy, tend to open up when influenced by a literary text. Studies have shown that bibliotherapy can in fact be particularly helpful for anyone with an avoidant attachment style.[26] Attachment styles are the ways in which people form and maintain emotional connections with others. They are shaped by our early childhood experiences with caregivers. There are four main attachment styles: secure (comfortable with intimacy, seeking out close relationships); anxious (overly dependent on their partners, worrying about rejection or abandonment); avoidant (strong desire for independence and autonomy, trusting others less and avoiding emotional intimacy); and disorganised (a combination of anxious and avoidant attachment styles, wanting intimacy but also unable to trust others, fearing rejection or abandonment). For someone with the avoidant attachment style, who has a strong desire for independence and autonomy, bibliotherapy gives them freedom to help themselves without always needing to seek professional help. For this reason, readers with this attachment style may be particularly drawn to bibliotherapy.

Bibliotherapy also affords the reader a level of autonomy, as they can control the pace of their session by taking a break from reading if they begin to feel emotionally overwhelmed. The reader can also use their imagination to reduce the intensity of an image triggered by a particular section of text.

Connection

Secondly connection is paramount. The reader needs to believe that their feelings are acknowledged and validated, as this fosters a sense of belonging. By establishing a connection with the author or the text, the reader will relax their defences and be more willing to explore the value of literary thinking, mirroring the bond of trust that needs to develop between client and therapist in a traditional therapy setting. The process should encourage the release of emotions that have been supressed, allowing the reader to regain a sense of agency so that they can become more self-aware and liberated, and ultimately find a way to move forward.

THE BIBLIOTHERAPY PROCESS

So, how does the process actually work? In a typical bibliotherapy session, I will begin by asking a series of questions that are designed to help me get to know the reader better, and that will inform the book-selection process. Here are some examples:

- What brings you to the therapy room, and what are you looking to explore?

- What are your reading preferences and habits? Including:
  ○ How much time do you have to read?
  ○ Which literary mediums do you prefer (such as paperbacks, hardbacks, eBooks)?
  ○ What are your favourite genres, books and authors?

I will also ask general questions to get a better sense of you as a person, and to help me find out anything else that might be useful for me to know.

Once I have all this information, I can start to curate a reading list that will address any issues that you might be dealing with. We will go into this process in greater detail in Part III.

Bibliotherapy Sessions

Based on the information provided in advance of the session and the responses to the questions above, I prepare a curated reading list (a 'book prescription') for the first session. During our initial fifty-minute meeting, I examine the client's issues in more detail and introduce them to their reading list, which, depending on what I've learned in the session, may be tweaked to better suit the client's needs. The client chooses one or two books from this list with the goal of reading these and engaging in literary journaling between sessions. Literary journaling involves jotting down any thoughts or moments of self-reflection that have been prompted by reading (see Chapter 3 for detailed guidance on how to engage with this bibliotherapy technique). Their literary journal entries are then shared with me, either between sessions or during the session, to guide the therapeutic process. The therapy process does not stop when you leave the therapy room, so this gives clients a chance to continue documenting and processing how they are feeling.

In further sessions, clients are introduced to other creative bibliotherapy techniques that can play an active part in therapeutic processing, such as writing letters, essays or poetry, as well as unstructured creative writing, narrative therapy and literary reflective practices – we will touch on these in more detail in later chapters.

LITERARY GENRES USED IN BIBLIOTHERAPY

The texts used in bibliotherapy can be fiction or non-fiction, and can take many forms, from novels to poetry, plays to memoirs, and self-help books to essays. While works of fiction tend to move us more, some non-fiction – particularly narrative works such as memoir and biography – can have a similar effect. Just remember when picking a book that the most important thing is for it to align with the reader's preferences, as this will influence how well the reader connects with the text, and in turn with their own feelings and thoughts. There will be readers who connect with Greek tragedy, or with graphic novels, or with spiritual texts – and everything in between. Different genres serve a purpose, and it is my role as a bibliotherapist to leverage the therapeutic interventions they provide.

THE ART OF LITERARY CURATION

Now that you have a better understanding of how bibliotherapy works, you might be wondering how to go about curating a list of therapeutic texts (and we'll look at the process in more detail in Part III). The focus of my work will always be my clients – what issues are they bringing to our sessions? Which literary character or story do they need to connect with? What is the literary medium or construct that will make them feel at home, at ease, just like they would in a therapist's office?

I have had clients who have been grieving their spouses, and have found comfort in the *Beginner's Goodbye* by Anne Tyler and Joan Didion's *The Year of Magical Thinking*. I have worked with divorcees who have found solace in Rachel Cusk's *Aftermath* and Florence Williams's *Heartbreak*. I have seen trauma sufferers gain insight and relief from Bessel Van Der Kolk's *The Body Keeps the Score*, Arundhati Roy's *The God of Small Things* and Virginia Woolf's *Mrs Dalloway*.

In the following chapters, I'll cover their journeys of healing, of finding themselves, and of discovering meaning, purpose and peace – and, most importantly, their small epiphanies of life-changing wisdom and the bibliotherapy techniques that made them possible. I'll also cover my own.

PART II

Bibliotherapy
Journeys

3

A BIBLIOTHERAPIST'S JOURNEY OF HEALING

'Some books seem like a key to unfamiliar rooms in one's own castle.'

FRANZ KAFKA AND RICHARD WINSTON, *LETTERS TO FRIENDS, FAMILY AND EDITORS (THE SCHOCKEN KAFKA LIBRARY)*

CHILDHOOD

My childhood memories of reading remain vivid. First, the soothing voices of my parents weaving together words and pictures to create colourful, spellbinding stories of courage and joy that teleported me to exciting far-flung locations. Later, when I learned to read by myself, I'd sit in a spacious oak cupboard, layered with pillows, and disappear into new worlds, like Lucy in *The Lion, the Witch and the Wardrobe*, although I never really left my cupboard. I understood the world through reading – and I knew I wasn't alone.

My memories of leafing through the pages of Jayne Fisher's *Garden Gang* books remain bright even after all these years. The characters, Penelope Strawberry, Roger Radish, Pam Parsnip and Lawrence Lemon, were all anthropomorphic fruits and vegetables. They had strong opinions and unique temperaments; Penelope Strawberry was vain and snobby, while Roger Radish was shy. When I look back at what drew me to these books, it was the sense of novelty, wonder and imagination. At four years old, who wouldn't want to live in a world of talking fruits and vegetables that took you on fascinating, fun-filled journeys, and who, like you, had their own insecurities or fears?

As a shy child, it felt safe and comforting to read about Roger Radish overcoming his shyness – with a little help from a forceful wizard – to save some drowning chives. Each of the *Garden Gang* stories usually started with a small problem that evolved into a challenge of mighty proportions for the daring fruit or vegetable to resolve, transforming them into a hero in the process. This 'problem, resolution and transformation-to-hero' arc resonates with children just as much as it does with adults; so much so, in fact, that the writer Joseph Campbell came up with a theory to explain it. In *The Hero with a Thousand Faces*, Campbell explained that the archetypal hero's journey could be broken down into three stages: first, the hero has to change their existing situation in response to a threat or challenge, with the hope that doing so will improve their life; second, the hero will experience a moment of divine realisation that will allow them to overcome the challenge they are facing; finally, the hero can return home with newfound wisdom, perspective and insight. This journey is appealing because it gives us hope and inspires us to navigate our own worries, knowing that we can arrive at a better outcome.

As I got a bit older, I moved on from the *Garden Gang* and fell in love with Enid Blyton's *The Faraway Tree*, a series of books revolving around children who discover an enchanted tree that acts as a gateway to other magical lands and is home to fairy-folk. These books were so beautifully imaginative that I found myself transported to a charming world that I wanted to live in forever. Another firm favourite was Carolyn Keene's *Nancy Drew* series, which centred on the titular high-school detective. Every page fizzed with Nancy's courage and can-do attitude. Nancy went where other girls didn't dare. She solved puzzles and mysteries that even adults couldn't. She was a larger-than-life heroine, and gave me hope that I too could be just as ferociously brave.

In his book *The Dynamics of Literary Response*, academic and literary critic Norman Holland argued that all literature is children's literature, and that the better part of what we do when we read is activate emotional resonances between the text and our unacknowledged fantasies of returning to 'pre-Oedipal' pleasures. In classical psychoanalytic theory, this refers to the sensory and emotional pleasures experienced during the early stages of a child's development, specifically with regards to their relationship with their mother or primary caregiver.

This echoes William Wordsworth, who famously included the line 'The Child is father of the Man' in his poem 'My Heart Leaps Up'. The line suggests that the experiences and behaviours we develop in childhood shape who we become as adults, and it is often interpreted as emphasising the importance of childhood experiences in shaping our personalities, beliefs and attitudes. This idea has been adopted in psychoanalytic theory, particularly in the work of Sigmund Freud and his followers.

TEENAGE LIFE

Judy Blume and George Eliot created platforms for parallel lives, allowing me as a teenager to live both in the worlds of their stories, and in my own reality. They got me through the shock of starting my menstrual cycle. I felt deeply ashamed when it happened (partly because in Hinduism and Jainism, my birth religions, it was viewed as the time of the month when you're 'not clean'). Reading about Margaret's experience in *Are You There God? It's Me, Margaret* reassured me that how I felt and what I felt was completely normal – and that extended to the ambivalent feelings I had towards boys, too. Judy Blume was a literary fairy godmother whose books were spells that made everything okay in the end, and made puberty at least bearable.

I read George Eliot in my teens for my English Literature GCSE course, and was unconsciously drawn to the psychological depths of her characters – although I didn't really understand what psychology was, or that her writing could be described as such. A proto-psychologist, Eliot's characters were multi-dimensional, full of conflict and cognitive dissonance that felt like terrifyingly accurate depictions of the human condition. I found her writing so relatable that I wanted to stay in the pages for as long as I could, and it felt almost as if she was writing about me. Here was someone who understood my pain, and her writing allowed me to be vulnerable without feeling exposed.

Eliot's *Mill on the Floss* takes place during the early nineteenth century, and centres around Maggie Tulliver, a clever, idealistic young woman growing up in a patriarchal society. From a young age, Maggie craves the approval of her pragmatic, steady older brother, Tom. The siblings share a close yet fraught bond that is tested by their opposing natures and societal expectations, and, as they mature, Tom becomes increasingly distant and withholding of his affection. This has a major influence on Maggie, ultimately driving her to constantly seek approval from the people around her in later life. Maggie's pattern of behaviour is a striking example of Eliot's understanding of how our childhood relationships can impact our lives as adults, and as we have seen, her writing even inspired some of Freud's own theories about human development and the influence of childhood experience.

For me, *Mill on the Floss* emphasised that it's not always possible to get the approval we seek from relatives, friends, teachers and authority figures. But why do we need their approval in the first place? As a people-pleaser myself, I intimately understood Maggie's desperate need for her brother's acknowledgement. If we are repeatedly denied the assurance of the people around us, the fear of getting things wrong, making mistakes and ultimately being rejected or disliked by others begins to settle in, and we can begin to fear that we don't belong. This need for belonging is primal, and if it goes unmet, it can cause all sorts of anxieties. I remember my teenage self wanting to comfort Maggie and to let her know that she didn't need her brother's approval. I wanted to support Maggie and show her how he was holding her back. But was my heart aching for Maggie, or was I trying to comfort myself? I was so decisive when it came to what Maggie needed, yet at the same time, I was unaware of how I was standing in my own way. It was like looking into a mirror, and it made me realise that I was holding myself back. I asked myself, how could I stop this desperate need for approval? The first step was really the awareness and recognition of it. The second step was practising self-compassion and reinforcing my own value, which was not based on someone else's scale of how much they liked me or disliked me, or how likely they were to reject my views. *The Mill on the Floss* was a torch in the dark for me; it revealed to me that I had an inner life that had been previously plagued by anxiety and fear. I learned that this was normal. I also realised how vulnerable and conflicted we all are.

EARLY ADULTHOOD

Reading continued to be a sanctuary for me in early adulthood. I loved that books afforded me the opportunity to live vicarious existences in imagined worlds where the meaning of life could be tested in a safe way, incubating us from the trials of real life, which often felt daunting, difficult or fatiguing. These books were a portal to a safer world, one that was more compassionate and understanding: a place where I could sit with my pain, let it be held, so that I could look at it with clear eyes again, and eventually release it.

In hindsight, I have lived half my life in the pages of books, relying on them to put my real life into perspective. Sometimes, doing this has shifted how I view the real world. I realise that living in these two worlds side by side has enabled me to live a life enchanted by reading, and it has also helped me heal when life's cracks have abruptly showed up. I wouldn't have it any other way.

In 1996, my parents, my brother and I immigrated to the UK, where I completed my A levels at a school in Hertfordshire. Despite literature being my first love, I went on to study mathematics at university, before landing at a major auditing firm and then moving into investment banking. Just a few years of working in the banking industry took a huge toll on my health. My job as a risk analyst involved long hours, and while it was interesting, it was by no means fulfilling – and no amount of money could justify the level of stress it caused. I found that I wanted to swap advising investment banking clients on how to manage their risk to maximise profit for advising people on how to manage their pain for emotional freedom. I knew I wanted to pursue something more meaningful than finance, and I had always been drawn towards understanding people – what makes them tick, how they work and how they can improve their lives – so I decided to study psychodynamic counselling.

As I mentioned earlier, undergoing personal therapy is a prerequisite when you're training to be a counsellor, so this also meant that for the first time, I would have to openly share my thoughts with a stranger. Once I was introduced to bibliotherapy, I began to lean increasingly on literature and poetry as my form of emotional support. In between therapy sessions, I would turn to literature as a prompt for journaling and self-reflection ('literary journaling') and this quickly became a daily ritual.

LITERARY JOURNALING: HOW IT WORKS

Literary journaling requires us to keep a journal of all the books we've read and the impact they've had on us. Journaling is one of the best ways to connect with ourselves, reflect on our emotions and thoughts, and gain some clarity amidst the day-to-day stresses and strains of life. It brings a feeling of calm and helps us to make sense of the world and ourselves.

Writing down the emotions a piece of literature triggers, good or bad, can be very beneficial, particularly when working through negative feelings. As author and theoretical physicist Leonard Mlodinow discusses in his book *Emotional: The New Thinking About Feelings*, expressing unwanted, negative emotion helps to relieve it. It has the same effect as increasing your brain activity in the prefrontal cortex (the part of the brain responsible for key cognitive abilities such as executive function, including decision-making and problem-solving, as well as creativity and perseverance), and decreasing activity in the amygdala (the part responsible for processing fearful and threatening stimuli) by reducing the fear and anxiety response, leading to better emotional regulation.

Emotional regulation is an essential part of daily functioning and well-being, and involves being able to navigate both our positive and negative emotions in a helpful way that does not leave us feeling overwhelmed or so consumed by emotion that we cannot function optimally on a daily basis. This results in better decision-making and resilience, and prevents the exacerbation of mental health conditions such as anxiety and depression. It also allows us to navigate conflict and communicate effectively.

Writing about upsetting experiences has also been shown to reduce high blood pressure, lessen chronic pain symptoms, improved mood and sleep, and boost immune function.[27] As Shakespeare writes in *Macbeth*, 'Give sorrow words. The grief that does not speak whispers the o'er-fraught heart, and bids it break.'

When we journal, we are encouraged to investigate why a particular character, situation or even style of writing might provoke in us a sense of joy, disgust, trepidation, fury, comfort, and so on. Reading can bring out emotions that we haven't felt for some time, so it's important to journal in order to process them. In doing so, we can pay closer attention to our emotions, get to know ourselves better, and delve deeper into our colourful inner worlds.

Literature affords us a certain power in terms of what it enables us to explore, access and draw on. The goal of literary journaling is to unleash this power and bring forth the unconscious into the conscious. It offers a different approach to self-therapy,* one which, if leveraged correctly, can offer new ways of seeing and being, allowing us to adopt a more flexible approach to life's daily challenges and to build resilience and inner confidence.

A question I'm often asked is: 'How do I start?' There is no right or wrong answer, but I've found the following three-step process incredibly effective:

1) Select Literature You Truly Connect With

- Is there an area in your life that you'd like to work on or explore further, or an issue you are currently facing (for example, loss, anxiety, imposter syndrome, boundary-setting)?
- Is there a movement that you are particularly interested in, or a cultural issue you are curious about?
- Is there a book you're currently reading that you're connecting with, or something you've read in the past that has truly moved you, or that you want to find out

---

*   'Self-therapy' refers to the practice of individuals engaging in therapeutic activities or techniques to address their emotional, psychological, or behavioural challenges on their own, without the direct involvement of a licensed therapist or mental health professional. It's important to note that while self-therapy can be beneficial for some individuals in certain situations, it may not be suitable for everyone or all mental health concerns. In more severe cases or when dealing with complex issues, seeking professional help from a qualified therapist or counsellor is often recommended. Self-therapy can complement traditional therapy or serve as a useful tool for personal growth and self-awareness when used responsibly and judiciously.

more about? This could be the subject, the author or the characters.

Find a book that addresses the above, and consider the following:

- What genres do I enjoy reading? Fiction (such as historical fiction, literary fiction, mystery)? Non-fiction (such as memoir, biography, essays)? Poetry?
- What writing style do I prefer?
- How much time can I devote to reading each week? (If you're running low on time, consider a short story or essay collection versus a longer novel or memoir.)
- What reading medium is the book available in? (Don't feel constrained to physical editions, as you may prefer to opt for an eBook or audiobook instead.)
- If you have a shortlist in mind, you may want to narrow it down by asking yourself whether all the books you are considering provide the level of diversity or representation that you're looking for.

You might also find the 'Matching Reader Personality to Genre' quiz on pages 92–5 helpful.

Once you have chosen a book, follow steps 2 and 3 below to kickstart the journaling process.

2) Highlight, Journal and Reflect

Highlight passages or make notes of any lines you've loved, write down how they made you feel, and consider the possible reasons for why the text resonated with you. You may want to sleep on your thoughts and come back to them the next day to see if you still feel the same way. If you do, then this might be something you need to explore further, potentially in therapy or with a book that covers this issue in more detail. Alternatively, discuss what you've read with a friend or family member, as this can be a good way to organise your thoughts, and they may offer a new perspective that can lead to more prompts. Discussing these in a bibliotherapy or therapy session might also invite further insight.

On the other hand, if you've taken some time to reflect on your journal entry and your thoughts have now changed, ask yourself what exactly has changed. Have you reached a resolution? What does this tell you about yourself? Have you learned a lesson? Do you need to explore a new avenue, or are you ready to move on?

3) Consolidate

Consolidating your thoughts and feelings will bring a conclusion that's often forgotten when we journal. This is a significant part of the journaling process. Think of it as a way

> to tie together all the thoughts and feelings that a piece of
> writing might have provoked in you, so that you can consider
> what you've learned about yourself with clarity. This import-
> ant step weaves together your story with your reading, and
> illuminates your destination.

Exploring Boundaries Through Books and Literary Journaling

My biggest lesson during my therapy sessions was how to set boundaries, something I had never been taught. To understand what I mean,
we have to travel back in time to 1980s Nairobi, Kenya, where I grew
up. My parents are second-generation Gujarati, Indian immigrants.
There was a big community of us across East Africa, but the one in
Nairobi was the largest. Hardworking, entrepreneurial and ambi-
tious, the first generation risked everything and traversed the Indian
Ocean by boat in the early 1900s, despite not knowing whether they'd
even survive the journey due to disease and food shortages. Yet they
survived, and even flourished. They established thriving businesses
and operated farms and factories, setting future generations up for
success. The single most important contributing factor was the close-
knit community they formed. People helped each other to settle into
their new homes, build businesses and positively collaborate.

There's always a trade-off, though. Communal spirit also bred
orthodoxy. Issues like bullying, depression, dealing with teen angst,
navigating relationships and sex education were considered out of
bounds. Conversations around mental health were unheard of, and

there was no access to any form of support or therapy. For me, books filled this gap, and reading was the closest I came to feeling supported in my mental well-being.

If someone within the community exhibited signs of depression or anxiety, the response was often to hide them away and keep their struggle secret to avoid risking shame. Depression and other mental health conditions were little understood. The fear of shame – *What would people think?* – was instilled in each of us, and stopped us from being our most authentic selves. We created a society of people-pleasers. The ripest space for anxiety to rear its head. And guilt, too.

Strong, thriving communities tend to be collectivist in nature, and people brought up in collectivist societies are more attuned to thinking about the group rather than the self. Difficulty in differentiating the self from the community can make it hard when it comes to setting boundaries. This is something I struggled with. I'd been aware of the role I was primed to play for as long as I could remember: to be a good daughter, even if it meant putting aside my own desires, and to always prioritise communal goals over personal ones. I often felt enmeshed. I'd feel guilty if I did something that went against what my family wanted, even if it was something important to me. And I'd feel guilty for setting a boundary that allowed me to feel safe, if doing so also meant that I could risk upsetting other members of my family or community. This difficulty with setting boundaries would overwhelm my work and relationships in my twenties, despite me no longer being tied to the community in East Africa. It was only once I learned how to navigate these through my training as a counsellor, and through literature, that things began to feel lighter, more manageable.

I linked my difficulty to set boundaries to my desire to please others – I was a people-pleaser. To be honest, I had no idea what 'boundaries' even meant in an emotional context until I started my training and explored them further in therapy sessions. Even then, I struggled to introduce healthy boundaries into my own life. My inability to say 'no', and the guilt that followed if I did, meant that I took on more than I could manage at work and struggled with episodes of chronic stress, with the symptoms manifesting both mentally and physically. During my accountancy training, I felt overwhelmed, stressed and burned out, and eventually began to experience panic attacks about going into work. I could not face another day in the office. I was diagnosed with irritable bowel syndrome. I lost considerable weight and eventually left the job – ironically, to join an even more aggressive investment bank, where I completed my accountancy training. And so the difficulties with boundary-setting persisted.

It was Anne Katherine's book *Where to Draw the Line* that really helped me to understand healthy boundary-setting. Her stories of people who had struggled with boundaries and had successfully managed to let go of their people-pleasing tendencies made me feel optimistic that I could do it too. She wrote practical examples of how to *actually* set them. In theory, boundary-setting seemed straightforward, but the application of it often felt hopeless. I was convinced that I would never be someone who could assert themselves without feeling guilty when they needed to say no to a work project, or who could ask for more time when making a decision, or who could respectfully let their family know that they needed space. But I discovered that change was possible, regardless of the difficult spaces and narratives in which we find ourselves. As a people-pleaser, you learn to please everyone around you but yourself. Acknowledging that I had the agency to please myself first, before worrying about the needs of others, was life-changing. Although I often felt guilty for putting my own needs first, by working through my concerns through literary journaling, I found I could accept this new way of being.

I can now see red flags as soon as they appear. If something feels odd or strange, I don't gloss over it, I stop and pay attention to it. In the past, I would convince myself that *I* was the problem. A partner dismissing my emotions as me being oversensitive, a friend repeatedly showing up late, another friend only getting in touch when they needed something: these were all red flags that I should have heeded. My boundaries were not being respected – perhaps because I was not setting them. I was not saying, 'It's not okay to treat me like this.' By staying silent, I was participating in my own boundary violation.

Learning to recognise boundary violations was important, but even once I had, it was still difficult for me to voice my feelings due to a fear of rejection and a sense of guilt around hurting someone else's feelings. I knew that I had to do something about these emotions. As Anne Katherine writes in *Where to Draw the Line*, 'The longer we stay in a violating situation the more traumatised we become. If we don't act on our own behalf, we will lose spirit, resourcefulness, energy, health, perspective, resilience. We must take ourselves out of violating situations for the sake of our wholeness.'

Having worked a great deal with clients on fear and anxiety in the therapy room, I knew that one of the best ways to deal with fear was to accept it, honour it and then face it. For the sake of my inner peace and mental well-being, I had to let others know how I felt in the hope that my feelings would be acknowledged and their behaviour would change for the better. My guilt stemmed from my tendency to put the needs of others over my own, and I knew I had to put myself first and honour what I needed. To do otherwise would be a betrayal.

After journaling on the idea of setting healthier boundaries, I put what I'd learned into practice. And remarkably, there were friends and relatives who changed their behaviour to accommodate my newly set boundaries – they heard me and respected my needs. Of course, there were also those who didn't, and this process helped me to identify them and weed them out. Suddenly, life started to feel less complicated and overwhelming, although it was bittersweet, as I had to let go of some relationships that had been a key part of my life. It was messy and hard at times, but once I had mourned these losses, I realised I could make peace with them and move on.

ADULTHOOD

After therapy and becoming a parent, I'd made leaps and bounds in boundary-setting, yet there was still something niggling at me. Something was missing. It wasn't until I read Toni Morrison's *The Bluest Eye* that I realised what it was. In the book, Morrison confronts racism within the Black community, the struggle of being a woman in a patriarchal society, and class dynamics, all of which felt incredibly familiar to me. Although deeply disturbing, Morrison's writing resonated with me, and I felt that she astutely captured emotions that we all experience, although in perhaps less violent ways, from never feeling good enough and being othered to our longing to be loved and accepted for who we are. In the novel, Pecola's desire for blue eyes rather than brown ones not only highlights the racism that she has internalised, but also emphasises her longing to be truly seen by those around her. For Pecola, blue eyes are symbolic of beauty, and of the love, respect and acceptance she so craves.

Pecola's story reminded me of my own invisibility growing up, as a girl in an East African Indian community, where there was a clear division between the women and men – the men were seen as superior. When boys were born, their mothers were celebrated; when girls were born, their mothers were consoled. Women would do all the cooking and cleaning, while the men relaxed in the living room and engaged in intellectual conversations. Although girls were sent to schools and prestigious universities overseas, their primary duty was still to serve the needs of men. For women, marriage often meant swapping career prospects for the joys of being a housewife. At least, this was what was modelled by the women in our community in my late teens and early adulthood. And, in a similar vein to the pursuit of 'whiteness' experienced by Pecola, in our community there was also a bias towards being 'fair and lovely'. To be slightly darker-skinned as a woman was frowned upon, so you would avoid tanning at all costs – which, in sunny Kenya, proved challenging.

This is where I found Morrison's writing helpful. The experiences of Pecola and other female characters in the novel highlighted the intersection of sexism and racism: the ways in which society's expectations of beauty and femininity can be oppressive and harmful, particularly for women of colour, creating and sustaining power imbalances that contribute to the marginalisation and subservience of women, particularly for those who do not conform to traditional beauty standards.

There was also the question of social capital and status: how wealthy was your family and how many siblings did you have? Did you have a large extended family? The larger your family, the higher your social standing and social capital, and the more valued you were, as connections were currency. Growing up, these beliefs and silent social structures took root. I never felt good enough: I came from a smallish family; I was female and measured somewhere in the middle on the whiteness spectrum. These pervasive ideas followed me from the past into the present, and even as an adult, the feeling of invisibility managed to filter into many of my relationships and experiences. I carried with me the conviction that I didn't matter. Over the years, the community has evolved – there's not much of a 'fair and lovely' culture anymore, and it's a lot less patriarchal – but the seeds of invisibility from my younger years have been firmly sown within.

The sense of not feeling seen was also compounded by my professional environment. When I worked in finance in London, a patriarchal culture still existed and the office was predominantly white and male (although now there's more diversity and inclusion initiatives in place). Sometimes, I would walk into a meeting room and say a bold hello, but people would either look straight through me, or their body language would indicate their dismissiveness. The message seemed to be that there was no space here for a petite British Indian female. The same was true for other non-white female minorities. It was an incredibly difficult world to exist in.

I want to share a reflection from my journal after reading *The Bluest Eye*, which I think gives a sense of how the book helped to crystallise and acknowledge my feelings:

Of all the things that have troubled me in relationships, setting appropriate boundaries, 'being too nice' and always putting others' needs in front of mine, the thing that's persisted is this deep desire to be seen, to be visibly available to others. Pecola's experience, while extreme, reminds us how deeply the communities we are raised in can haunt us, their power omnipresent, affecting how we experience the world for the rest of our lives. To the point that we unconsciously attract the same types of communities in later life, whether that's friendship groups or work cultures, where the familiarity of invisibility is more comfortable than taking up space, which can sometimes feel unnerving.

The wish to be seen, to be heard, to be witnessed is primal. Those of us who grew up meeting the needs of others (often those of men) and putting the needs of others before our own can frequently end up feeling like we've never been acknowledged and that our emotions, needs and desires were neglected. As seedlings, we were left to fend for ourselves under the scorched sun without adequate nourishment and care.

AUDIO-JOURNALING

Although I understood what motivated my desire to be seen, the problem lay in 'fixing' it. The emptiness refused to go away. I was navigating a path with a starless sky. This time, instead of writing down my thoughts, I audio-journaled. I began to leave myself voice notes. I told my inner child, who had felt neglected for so long, that I was there for her. That I understood her pain. That I was sorry she felt so alone. I cried. I let myself feel the pain, the sadness, the hurt, the abandonment, the fear: all the emotions from my childhood that I hadn't fully resolved.

AUDIO-JOURNALING: HOW IT WORKS

The beauty of audio-journaling is that you can capture your raw emotions in their purest form as you experience them. A voice note is an accurate snapshot of how you feel in the moment, and it can offer a way for you to release your frustration, fear and anger, and channel these emotions into something more productive instead.

Physiologically, when we give voice to our feelings, our tense muscles loosen up. There's a mental and physical sensation of releasing pent-up emotion. You start to make sense of what you journaled and your feelings. Suddenly, the important things stand out. There's more clarity than there was before.

Recently, audio-journaling has also been recognised as a helpful reflective practice by various researchers in New York, who have worked with teenagers in Jerusalem, Gaza and New York City to record their experiences of audio-journaling for self-reflection.[28]

How Does Audio Journaling Differ from Literary Journaling?

Audio-journaling will appeal to anyone who finds it easier to verbalise their thoughts rather than organise them on the page. It's also a good technique for people who are more auditory than visual, who find it easier to absorb information through listening rather than seeing. It is particularly helpful for those with lower literacy, linguistic difficulties or disability.

Listening back to your audio recordings will allow you to feel that your voice has been heard, understood, acknowledged and validated in a literal sense, something you might not experience as viscerally when rereading your journal entries.

Audio-journaling also captures the emotional context of a statement, which is often missing in the written word. For example, 'I need to change' can be interpreted in many different ways on the page, but a voice note offers an indication of the intention behind the words.

Practising audio-journaling allowed me to release the pain I was holding. I was relieved of it and able to move on. Listening back to the voice notes, the older me was paying witness to this pain. I felt safe, as if my feelings were acknowledged and even understood. Listening back to difficult feelings signalled to my brain that I had been heard – I didn't need someone else to hear these or listen to me. I could let go of these feelings. This self-validation was both liberating and healing. I began to grow taller. My shoulders were less slumped; my body relaxed. Psychologically and physiologically, I felt lighter. I wasn't hiding anymore. I was letting myself take up space.

AFFIRMATIONS

Words have always saved me – whether as a form of self-expression or as a way to build self-esteem or reinforce and cultivate a more positive outlook on life – and I think this is why I've found positive affirmations to be such a powerful tool too. By 'positive affirmations', I mean simple statements, such as:

'I matter.'
'What I'm feeling matters.'
'My presence is valued.'
'I am worthy of unconditional love and affection.'
'I am healing.'
'My needs are important, and I must honour them.'

POSITIVE AFFIRMATIONS – HOW IT WORKS

Positive affirmations are statements used to reinforce positive beliefs or attitudes about oneself, others or the world. The idea behind using positive affirmations is that by consistently repeating them, they can help to shift one's mindset and cultivate a more positive outlook. A 2013 article by David K. Sherman that consolidates various studies on the use of affirmations found that positive affirmations can reduce the stressful impact of challenges and threats in our lives, and that this can have a long-lasting effect.[29]

To use positive affirmations effectively, it's important to choose statements that resonate with you personally and that reflect the type of mindset or attitude you want to cultivate. Some people find it helpful to repeat their affirmations out loud several times a day, while others prefer to write them down or visualise them in their mind. The practice can take time to have a noticeable effect on our self-esteem, mindset and outlook, so it's important to be patient and use them consistently.

I relied on affirmations and audio-journaling extensively during my own therapy while training (prior to leaving banking). I considered these to be active techniques versus passive ones. Active techniques, such as journaling and role-playing, require the client's active participation and engagement in the therapeutic process. Passive techniques involve the client being more of a recipient of the therapeutic intervention, such as guided imagery visualisation or, in the case of bibliotherapy, reading without applying any additional bibliotherapy techniques. Both active and passive techniques have a place in therapy. In bibliotherapy, I find that active techniques complement the more passive activity of reading, enabling and empowering the participant to get the most out of their reading.

Affirmations and audio-journaling became lifelines, and I've continued to use both ever since. A few years ago, my husband's job meant that we had to relocate to San Francisco for two years.

Even after I qualified as a counsellor, I had continued to work in investment banking. On the side, though, I had been slowly developing my bibliotherapy practice, and in 2017, when we moved to San Francisco, I finally felt ready to leave banking and devote myself to bibliotherapy full-time. Initially, I was often alone at home with a young baby while expecting a second, and there were times when I felt isolated and homesick, but these *active* techniques saved me again and again by soothing my uncertainty and anxiety.

LITERARY REFLECTIVE PRACTICE

Another active technique I have found helpful for building self-awareness (particularly when it comes to emotions and thoughts) and problem-solving, is what I call 'literary reflective practice'.

LITERARY REFLECTIVE PRACTICE – HOW IT WORKS

As the name suggests, this approach involves reflecting on what you've read and then using your newfound insight to work out what your needs and goals are. You can then put together an action plan for your personal development, monitoring and measuring your progress in meeting these needs and achieving these goals.

Although literary reflective practice shares some

---

similarities with literary journaling, one of the key differences is that it offers a more structured, goal-orientated approach to working through the thoughts and feelings that a text might elicit, whereas journaling is a freer form of expressive writing that can act as a release for pent-up emotion. I see literary reflective practice as an ideal framework for self-improvement, and journaling as perfect for self-expression.

Literary Reflective Practice Framework

To engage in literary reflective practice, use the following framework and structure:

- Select a text (poem, novel, memoir, graphic novel or any other genre) based on a theme or issue that you want to explore further. (Refer to Chapter 11: Selecting a Book for more details on how to select a text.)
- Reflect on what feelings the characters or story are triggering in you, what insights you might have gained and any lessons you have taken away from the story.
- You may also want to discuss the reflections you capture above in a counselling, therapy or bibliotherapy session, or discuss with a friend or family member to gain different perspectives or insights.
- Based on these reflections and discussions, identify what you need and what your goals are.

- Create a plan with action points to achieve these goals.
- Monitor, measure and evaluate your progress.

Refer to Chapters 5, 9 and 10 for more details of how this is used in practice.

GRATITUDE

Gratitude is a powerful, welcome emotion that can instantly uplift us. A 2015 study conducted by researchers and neuroscientists at the Brain and Creativity Institute at the University of Southern California[30] concluded that immersing ourselves in other people's stories of expressing gratitude helps us to feel more grateful in our own lives (refer to 'Reading Gratitude Narratives – How It Works' on page 76 for more details of this study).

I maintain a weekly gratitude practice where I reread passages from three powerful gratitude narratives.* My go-to titles include *Little Women* by Louisa May Alcott, *The Choice* by Edith Eger and *The Nightingale* by Kristin Hannah. Although each of these books spans different genres and periods of history, they all reiterate to me the power of gratitude in helping to find hope and joy even in the midst of great adversity. Reading about people who are able to be thankful and continue living despite extreme adversity helps me to feel less alone and encourages me to be more thankful for all of the things that I've taken for granted in my own life.

---

*   To keep things interesting, I also add new books or stories that I've come across during the week.

In a second study,[31] conducted in 2021, a group of female participants were asked to engage in a regular gratitude practice that involved writing about the people in their lives whom they were grateful towards. Images of the participants' brain activity after engaging in the writing exercise showed a reduction of activity in the amygdala, the part of our brain that responds to fear and anxiety. The results of the study suggested that practising gratitude can activate neural pathways associated with reward, pleasure and positive emotions and in turn these pathways dampen the activity of the amygdala, leading to a decrease in fear-related responses. Researchers also took blood samples to assess for inflammatory markers, noting an overall reduction of inflammation in the body, and measured the women's stress and anxiety levels, which decreased after writing. These findings strongly suggest that a gratitude practice can be hugely beneficial to our mental health and well-being.

READING GRATITUDE NARRATIVES – HOW IT WORKS

Participants in the 2015 Brain and Creativity Institute study were asked to watch a series of short documentaries that depicted the stories of Holocaust survivors.[32] They were then invited to read statements that would encourage them to imagine what their experiences as Holocaust survivors who had received life-saving assistance from a good Samaritan would look like; for example, 'You have been sick for weeks. A prisoner who is a doctor finds medicine and saves your life.'

To test the power of gratitude, scientists used fMRI (functional magnetic resonance imaging) to capture scans of the participants' brain activity in order to gauge their reactions to the documentaries and subsequent statements. The fMRI images showed that when the participants imagined an act of kindness from a good Samaritan, the regions of their brains associated with feeling gratitude lit up, as if they had actually experienced the gesture. This suggests that empathising with another's experience (in this case it was through the medium of film, but the same principle can be observed when reading) can elicit in us real feelings of gratitude.

To engage in this practice, select gratitude narratives or stories that speak to you and read these as regularly as you can. This could be weekly, fortnightly or monthly, depending on what works for you. It might also be helpful to keep an emergency to-be-read list for when you're feeling low or sad (see pages 234–293 for reading prescriptions).

GRIEF AND POETRY

Our stay in San Francisco came to an end eight months before Covid-19 struck, and we returned to London permanently. Unfortunately, during the pandemic, my paternal grandmother, who still lived in Kenya, passed away. Only three years earlier, I had lost my maternal grandmother, and now I was faced with another devastating loss, one that felt particularly acute. Despite our ambivalent relationships when I was a young child, my grandmothers had become incredibly important figures in my life, and as an adult I was very close to both of them. They had inspired in me a love of literature and language, as they devotedly read Gujarati newspapers, books and magazines. My memories of *Dadima* (my paternal grandmother) and *Nanima* (my maternal grandmother) will remain precious keepsakes.

Their deaths triggered a huge sense of loss, and reminded me that life is short. I needed a way to process my grief and, as always, I turned to reading. Psychotherapist Megan Devine's *It's OK That You're Not OK* guided me through my grief by showing me that it's possible for our loved ones to live on in us. If we look closely, we can see traces of them in everything that we do: in the ways we eat, live, think and write. My grief demanded a release, and so I gave voice to my pain through poetry:

> *Memories*
> *The memories have come to an end.*
> *With each passing day,*
> *They hold more significance,*
> *Like antiques, changing with time.*
> *Losing their accuracy,*
> *Their value and meaning overwhelming.*
>
> *We begin to remember them differently,*
> *Moulding them in our minds,*
> *Longing for those moments that bore the memory.*
> *Nostalgia blindsiding us.*

We begin to cherish them in a different way,
To perhaps how it really was.

They find permanence, in the geography of our minds.
Like fault lines, reminding us of our loss.
But also of our admiration for a person, a time and a
*   moment that is no more.*

I have found writing poetry hugely cathartic, as it's allowed me to make sense of my feelings on a given day, which is also why it's a particularly useful tool for processing grief.

WRITING POETRY – HOW IT WORKS

'Poetry is the spontaneous overflow of powerful feelings; it takes its origins from emotion recollected in tranquillity: the emotion is contemplated till by a species of reaction the tranquillity disappears, and an emotion, kindred to that which was before the subject of contemplation, is gradually produced, and does itself actually exist in the mind.'

WILLIAM WORDSWORTH

Poetry therapy is a form of expressive therapy that involves using poetry to promote emotional and psychological healing. It is based on the idea that reading, writing and discussing poetry can help individuals to explore their emotions, gain insight into their experiences, and develop a greater sense of self-awareness.

Poetry offers an opportunity to make a confession about something private or difficult, and often the best poems are written from the heart. It's a way to focus your mind, express your emotions and clarify your thoughts and feelings in a creative way. Once you've written your poem, you'll feel a welcome sense of calm that comes from no longer having to hold the burden of your confession.

If you're not used to writing your own poetry, you may find it difficult to get started, but it will become easier with practice. The key is to let your thoughts wander and write what comes to mind. Do not hold back; let go and allow the emotions, words and images to unfold. Sometimes, it's easier to write it all down first, before going back through what you've written and introducing line breaks and restructuring stanzas to make your poem more coherent – but it's also okay to keep your poems more abstract. A great book on writing poetry is *The Poet's Companion: A Guide to the Pleasures of Writing Poetry* by Kim Addonizio. It includes suggested writing themes and helpful techniques on how to deal with self-doubt and writer's block, as well as the highs and lows of writing life.

I wrote the poem on page 78, then left it for a couple of hours before rereading it to myself. The point is to take a break (this could be anything from a couple of hours to a few days) and then come back to it, to see if you feel the same or different.

The process felt ritualistic. With lit candles in the background as I read, I could sense the presence of my grandmothers in the shadows. My intuition spoke to me, reminding me I was not alone and that my grandmothers would always be a part of me. My mind turned to celebrated thinker Noam Chomsky's ideas on psychic continuity in the documentary *Is The Man Who Is Tall Happy?*[33] Chomsky asks what happens when we cut off a branch from a willow tree that is then put into the ground and grows into an identical replica of the original tree – is it still the same willow tree, or is it an entirely new one? Extending this analogy to humans, I wondered what happens to us when we are born: are we simply extensions of our parents and ancestors, or are we entirely new, separate entities in our own right? It's a question that's confounded for centuries. While I read my poem that night, I thought about my grandmothers. According to Jain and Hindu philosophy, their souls would be reincarnated – so would this mark a new beginning, the birth of entirely new identities, or would they simply live on as extensions of us, her family, upon reincarnation? I did not have all the answers, but I had literature to guide me and help me find meaning in my losses. I fell into deep introspection and reflection, re-evaluating what made my life more meaningful, and bibliotherapy was a big part of this introspection process. Word by word, sentence by sentence, I had processed emotion, grieved, and reorientated myself to live a more meaningful life. I felt fulfilled, yet I knew there was significantly more to do in this space. Part of this was to spread more awareness of bibliotherapy and its therapeutic benefits to readers everywhere. Some of them may also have found comfort and healing in books, but for a large majority, the concept of bibliotherapy still remained novel and unknown.

Bibliotherapy Toolkit

Bibliotherapy techniques used: Literary journaling, reading gratitude narratives, literary reflective practice, writing poetry.
Recommended for: Gratitude and relief from painful emotions.

Complementary therapeutic techniques: Audio-journaling, affirmations.
Recommended for: Feeling heard, understood and self-validation. Also helpful for empowerment and motivation.

Books read: Judy Blume's *Are You There, God? It's Me, Margaret,* George Eliot's *Mill on the Floss,* Anne Katherine's *Where to Draw the Line,* Tony Morrison's *The Bluest Eye,* Megan Devine's *It's OK That You're Not OK.*

BIBLIOTHERAPY TECHNIQUES APPLIED – KEY TAKEAWAYS & EXERCISES

Literary Journaling – Key Takeaways

- Keep a journal of all the books you've read and the impact they've had on you.
- Write down the emotions a piece of literature triggers, good or bad.

- Expressing unwanted negative emotions helps to relieve them through emotional regulation. Writing about upsetting experiences has also been shown to reduce high blood pressure, lessen chronic pain symptoms and boost immune function.
- Use the following process to guide you:
  - Choose literature that you connect with (use the **'Matching Reader Personality to Genre'** quiz on pages 92–3 to help you if you feel stuck).
  - Highlight, journal and reflect.
  - Consolidate your thoughts and feelings.

Exercise

Spend fifteen to thirty minutes journaling. Write whatever comes to mind; let the words and thoughts appear on paper. Here are some prompts to help you.

CHILDHOOD

Q1: What was your favourite book as a child?
PROMPT: What was it about this book that you connected with? Is there a part of this book that has shaped who you are now?

Q2: Was there a literary world in your childhood to which you wanted to escape?
PROMPT: What is it about this world that appeals?

Q3: Which book do you think should be taught to everyone at school?
PROMPT: Is this something you should revisit now?

EARLY ADULTHOOD
Q4: Was there a book series that you binge-read?
PROMPT: What did it feel like to lose yourself in a book?

Q5: Was there a book that you loved as a child or as a young adult?
PROMPT: Do you feel the same way about it or has it ruined your memory of it?

READING CURRENTLY
Q6: What book are you currently reading? What persuaded you to read it?
PROMPT: Was it the book cover? Or was it the blurb? Was it a recommendation from a friend?

Q7: If you were to write a book review of your favourite book, what would you write?
PROMPT: What resonated with you? Was there anything that left you slightly uncomfortable?

Q8: Do you tend to read one book at a time, or do you read multiple books at the same time?
PROMPT: Can you draw parallels between this answer and other areas of your life?

READING HIGHLIGHTS

Q9: What's your favourite comfort read?
PROMPT: What draws you to it?

Q10: Is there a passage from a book you would memorise in a heartbeat?
PROMPT: Why? What prominence does this passage have for you? Perhaps it's worth writing it out and placing it in a permanent space in your home.

PEOPLE

Q11: Have you ever enjoyed gossiping about book characters?
PROMPT: Gossiping sometimes unearths meaningful lessons – what have you learned from these characters and their behaviour? It might reveal something about yourself.

Q12: What non-fiction book has led you to discover somebody wonderful whom you had never come across before?
PROMPT: Why do you admire this person?

REVIEW

Q13: Go back and review your journal. How do you feel about your writing? Has anything changed? Is there a familiar pattern of behaviour that's repeating itself?
PROMPT: Reflect on what you've written and how you feel about it now. Write some action points for next steps.

Literary Reflective Practice – Key Takeaways

See 'Literary Reflective Practice Framework' on page 74.

Exercise

Reading and reflecting on poetry for stress relief has been very beneficial for my clients. One of my all-time favourite poems for stress relief is 'Leisure' by W. H. Davies:

> *What is this life if, full of care,*
> *We have no time to stand and stare?–*
>
> *No time to stand beneath the boughs*
> *   And stare as long as sheep or cows:*
>
> *No time to see, when woods we pass,*
> *   Where squirrels hide their nuts in grass:*
>
> *No time to see, in broad daylight,*
> *   Streams full of stars, like skies at night:*
>
> *No time to turn at Beauty's glance,*
> *   And watch her feet, how they can dance:*
>
> *No time to wait till her mouth can*
> *   Enrich that smile her eyes began?*
>
> *A poor life this if, full of care,*
> *   We have no time to stand and stare.*

What effect did the poem have on you? For me, the poem conjures images of springtime and facilitates a connection with nature. Yet it also feels bittersweet, as it laments how quickly life passes us by, and how sad it is when we are not truly living but just passing time. It urges us to stop and reconsider our lives. The sense of sadness and 'emptiness' it provokes makes us acknowledge the feelings held within us. It encourages us to enjoy the present moment and be more mindful. After these reflections, one of my goals was to spend more time in nature, taking in its beauty and enjoying the peace and calm that it can invoke.

You can use this exercise to explore other issues by selecting a poem or a poetry collection that's recommended for the themes you would like to focus on (see Chapter 12 for poetry recommendations categorised by mental health themes). Read and reflect on your chosen poem. What does the poem bring up for you?

Reading Gratitude Narratives – Key Takeaways

- By reading someone else's feel-good story of experiencing gratitude, we are also flooded with feelings of gratitude.
- There is a literal activation of circuits in the brain that help us feel more content and relaxed.
- Every week, fortnight or month (or whatever frequency works for you), select a narrative or story to read where the protagonist or author expresses gratitude.
- This can also be a helpful exercise when you're feeling low

or sad, so it might be helpful to keep an emergency 'to-be-read' list of gratitude stories for these moments.

Exercise

- Select a story or narrative where a protagonist or author expresses their gratitude. This could be a novel, a memoir, a short story or even a poem.
- Reflect on how reading such a story made you feel.
- A helpful book on writing poetry is *The Poet's Companion: A Guide to the Pleasures of Writing Poetry* by Kim Addonizio.

Writing Poetry – Key Takeaways

- Poetry offers an opportunity to make a confession about something private or difficult. Expressing unwanted emotions in this way relieves us so that we can move forward with clarity.
- Let your mind wander and write what comes to mind. Let your emotions, words and imagery come to life.
- You might find it easier to first write whatever comes to mind, and then structure the poem, introducing line breaks and stanzas.

Exercise

Here are some suggestions to get you started with your poem if you find yourself stuck.

- Name the emotion you are feeling and describe it in a four-line stanza.
- Talk about your fears.
- Talk about your losses.
- Talk about your dreams.
- Focus on a powerful image and describe it.
- Write about what inspires you.

COMPLEMENTARY THERAPEUTIC TECHNIQUES APPLIED – KEY TAKEAWAYS & EXERCISES

Audio-Journaling – Key Takeaways

- Audio-journaling captures your thoughts and feelings through recording your voice.
- Expressing your emotions in this way allows you to release emotions that might otherwise feel stuck.
- You feel heard, understood, acknowledged and validated.
- Physiologically, tense muscles loosen up, giving way to the physical and mental sensation of releasing pent-up emotion.
- You begin to make sense of what you journaled and your

feelings. The important things stand out. There's more clarity than there was before.

Exercise

- Whenever you're faced with a challenging emotion (sadness, overwhelm, anger or fear), record your feelings and thoughts over audio using a voice recorder or similar.
- Play back the voice note. How does it make you feel? Do you feel better after listening to your voice and your own emotions and thoughts? Does it make you feel lighter? Do you feel more enlightened or do you have a better idea of how to proceed with the possible dilemma or issue at hand?
- Repeat this audio-journaling practice a few times if necessary. Pay attention to strong emotions. Let them take up space and honour them. Often, we are tempted to ignore painful or difficult feelings, but this exercise is designed to make them easier to acknowledge and pay attention to. This is the start of the healing process: the release of these buried and stuck emotions.
- If helpful, further reflect on what you've heard. Have you changed your mind about how you felt? Do you now feel differently? Better? Or worse? Consolidate your reflections and learnings. If helpful, pull together a set of possible actions for next steps.

Positive Affirmations – Key Takeaways

- Positive affirmations are statements used to reinforce positive beliefs or attitudes about oneself, others or the world.
- Consistently repeating them can shift one's mindset, help cultivate a more positive outlook, and enable us to face challenges successfully.
- Choose statements that resonate with you personally and that reflect the type of mindset or attitude you want to cultivate.
- Repeat the affirmations out loud daily, or more frequently if necessary.
- Be patient and consistent as the practice can take time to have a noticeable effect.

Exercise

- Create a set of affirmations that support your goals and mental well-being for the future. Here are a few to help you get started:
  - *I value my body and I am grateful for all that it does for me.*
  - *I am stepping into the best version of myself every day.*
  - *I am supported by a wonderful set of relationships.*
  - *I deserve happiness, good health, and love.*
  - *I am doing something I love every day.*

- Work out how often you plan to say them out loud. It could be once a day, perhaps in the morning or just before bedtime. You may want to increase it to twice daily.
- Aim to create a long-term regular practice. Consistency is key.
- Adjust the affirmations if you need to, in response to changing circumstances.

Quiz: Matching Reader Personality to Genre

1. **What type of characters do you identify with or aspire to be like?**

   a. Characters who overcome adversity and demonstrate resilience.

   b. Characters who struggle with mental health issues and navigate their emotions.

   c. Characters who use humour to cope with difficult situations.

   d. Characters who find inner strength through their unique qualities or abilities.

2.   What type of conflict resonates with you the most?

    a.   Conflict related to trauma or difficult life experiences.

    b.   Conflict related to personal growth and self-discovery.

    c.   Conflict related to interpersonal relationships and communication.

    d.   Conflict related to feeling like an outsider or struggling with identity.

3.   What type of setting makes you feel safe and comfortable?

    a.   Realistic, familiar settings that remind you of home or places you know well.

    b.   Settings that reflect your cultural background or heritage.

    c.   Settings that are playful and imaginative, but still grounded in reality.

    d.   Settings that are completely different from your own experiences, allowing you to explore new perspectives and possibilities.

4. What type of themes resonate with you on a personal level?

   a. Themes related to overcoming adversity and building resilience.
   b. Themes related to mental health and self-care.
   c. Themes related to the power of laughter and finding joy in life.
   d. Themes related to finding inner strength and embracing unique qualities.

5. What type of emotions do you want to explore or process through reading?

   a. Feelings of fear or anxiety related to past traumas or difficult experiences.
   b. Feelings of uncertainty or confusion related to personal growth and change.
   c. Feelings of joy or happiness related to interpersonal relationships and connection.
   d. Feelings of empowerment or inspiration related to finding inner strength and embracing personal identity.

Results

Mostly As – Memoir, Autobiography or Self-help: Readers who identify with characters who have overcome adversity and demonstrate resilience may find inspiration and hope in reading memoirs, autobiographies or self-help books.

Mostly Bs – Young Adult or Contemporary Fiction: Readers who relate to characters who struggle with mental health issues or personal growth may benefit from reading young adult or contemporary fiction that explores the complexities of the human experience.

Mostly Cs – Humour: Readers who use humour to cope with difficult situations may find relief and comfort in reading humorous or light-hearted stories.

Mostly Ds – Fantasy or Science Fiction: Readers who find inner strength through their unique qualities or abilities may enjoy exploring new perspectives and possibilities through reading fantasy or science fiction stories.

These are general guidelines, and readers may find therapeutic value in multiple genres or themes. This quiz can help provide a starting point for readers who are looking for books to read that may resonate with them on a personal level.

4

TATYANA

> 'It is not death that a man should fear, but rather he
> should fear never beginning to live.'
>
> MARCUS AURELIUS, *MEDITATIONS*

---

*Client notes: Tatyana S. wants to process loss and depression
after being diagnosed with throat cancer. A memoir reader, she
wants to read about the experiences of other cancer sufferers.*

'Aleksei often used to tell me I was depressed. I barely left the
house. Instead, I'd get into my pyjamas, tuck myself into bed
and read.'

Thirty-seven-year-old Tatyana had been with her partner, Aleksei,
for six years when she came to see me. Tatyana had suffered from a
persistent sore throat, fatigue and a painful case of gastroesophageal
reflux, which she'd put down to her smoking habit and for which

she was also taking medication. By the time she was diagnosed, her cancer had reached Stage 4. Things at home were tense. There'd been a strain on the relationship even before the cancer, and the news of the diagnosis further exacerbated the discontent that Tatyana was already experiencing.

Tatyana and Aleksei had met at work. They were both IT consultants at a prestigious software company in London. The early stages of the relationship had been exciting, but with time, the spark between them had begun to flicker. Although marriage had been discussed more than once, neither Tatyana nor Aleksei had pursued it. The routine and monotony of the relationship had overshadowed the desire to move to the next stage, and they now felt that they had reached a crossroads where they would have to seriously consider the future of their relationship. Should they stay together?

It was a question that lingered in both of their minds, although it was not Tatyana's main focus, given her recent diagnosis. Her throat cancer – oesophageal cancer, to be precise – was aggressive. The doctors had told Tatyana that she only had up to a year left to live, and she was in complete disbelief. The whole situation felt surreal. She had never even considered that at thirty-seven, she could be so close to the end of her life.

Soon, the disbelief gave way to anger. Tatyana wanted answers; she wanted to know why this was happening to her. Faced with a terminal diagnosis, Tatyana had already started grieving the loss of her own life, navigating the five stages of grief: denial, anger, bargaining, depression and acceptance. She needed something to save her from the dark clouds engulfing her; something that would put an end to the 5am panic attacks she'd been experiencing. Part of her wanted to connect with other cancer sufferers. She wanted to ask them questions. But to connect with others would be to accept her diagnosis, and she wasn't quite ready to do that. Instead, Tatyana wanted to better understand her position through art, specifically literature, which is why she had come to see me.

'Since you enjoy reading memoirs, how about a memoir? It might feel safer, less intense, and perhaps might even validate some of your anxieties and concerns?' I suggested.

'That actually sounds great. I really need something that will help me make sense of everything that's going on at the moment,' Tatyana agreed. I could hear the hoarseness in her voice as she spoke. She cleared her throat. 'Knowing that I haven't got much longer to live is terrifying, and it's changed everything. I don't know what I should be doing anymore. I need to understand how other people got through this; how they managed to cope. I just can't help but feel so sad and empty.'

Tatyana's feelings were normal. It's common for cancer patients to seek out others who might be able to provide answers through their own lived experience.

'Can you talk to Aleksei about it? What are his thoughts?' I asked, wanting to learn a little more about the relationship at home and the impact this significant news was having.

'Yes, and no.' Tatyana hesitated, then continued. 'He has such a busy day job, and he's been teaching chess online in the evenings to try and save more money.'

I was a little bit concerned by this answer. 'Do you guys spend time talking to each other about your days?'

Tatyana responded reluctantly. 'We don't really spend much time talking, we just take each day as it comes. It's like we are housemates, each with our own lives.'

I felt a deep wave of sadness wash over me. It was becoming clear that something was not quite right.

Tatyana continued. 'We might as well not be in an intimate relationship. And now with the cancer, I don't really know where things will land. I don't think he even notices me anymore. You know, whether I look nice in something, or if I've had a haircut or made an extra effort.'

The loneliness in Tatyana's voice, coupled with the very painful cancer diagnosis, alarmed me.

'Do you tell him how you feel?' I asked gently.

'No, of course not. We've been together for so long, I'm sure he's sensed how I feel but he just isn't that bothered.'

I wasn't sure if that was entirely true, and wondered whether Aleksei just didn't know how to demonstrate that he cared.

Tatyana lowered her big brown eyes, accentuating the slight wrinkles on her forehead, she appeared to have aged beyond her years. She had withdrawn and seemed to have mentally shifted into her own world.

I had to bring her back to the present moment.

'Tell me about your childhood, Tatyana. Where did you grow up? What was your relationship with your parents like?'

'Oh, I grew up in St Petersburg with my grandparents. My father died when my sister and I were very young. I didn't really know him, and my mother and I haven't really spoken about it. There are some photos of us as all together as a family of four, and we look happy. When I was five and my sister three, my mother moved to London. She'd met someone British, so she decided to get a job here as a bookkeeper. And my sister and I joined her when we came to the UK for university. I got this job and ended up staying – and then, of course, I met Aleksei, and it made sense to be here.'

I could see from her resigned posture that she had accepted that this was how things were and how they would continue to be. She felt like an observer in her own life, and this had led to a feeling of resigned powerlessness that seemed to be serving her by keeping her relationship going and allowing things to remain as they were: stable. She seemed unwilling to rock the boat for fear of hitting rock bottom. This was her defence mechanism, and it had kept her afloat – until her cancer diagnosis.

I knew that not having her mother around during her formative years must have been extremely difficult for Tatyana. Absent parents can trigger a sense of abandonment that can linger for years and play havoc in our future relationships. Tatyana had chosen Aleksei, someone who was emotionally unavailable to her in many ways, and this mirrored her early relationship with her mother. In life, we tend to believe we deserve what we've always had. To alter these unhelpful and often harmful beliefs, we can turn to forms of therapy, including bibliotherapy. Through therapy, we can begin to unpick negative thought loops and welcome change, even though it almost always involves a loss of the familiar. And this loss can be painful, making the work of therapy harder.

I wanted Tatyana to know she was not alone in her predicament; others had walked this road, and had done so with courage and purpose amidst the challenges of living with cancer. I suggested Paul Kalanithi's book *When Breath Becomes Air*, the memoir of a neurosurgeon coming to terms with a terminal lung cancer diagnosis. This was the book we returned to in the majority of our sessions, along with Audre Lorde's *The Cancer Journals* and Louise Hay's *You Can Heal Your Life*. These books offered insight into the experience of cancer and the complexities it brings in a way that only literature and language can, by offering Tatyana the vocabulary to communicate what she might be going through. Through the stories and experiences of literary characters, we can gain inspiration and insight into our own struggles, and find the strength and courage to face our own challenges with greater self-understanding and self-compassion.

Conversations with friends and family, or even with a trained therapist, can still fail to recreate the artistic arrangement of language and experience that we can find in a book. Literature does not shy away from subjects that are difficult or painful to talk about, and instead offers a carefully thought-through, crafted message to gently awaken the reader to the underlying emotions they might be experiencing. Neurologically, our brains are wired to respond to narratives, as stories activate multiple regions of the brain involved in language processing, sensory perception and emotion regulation.[34] When we hear a story, our brains simulate the experiences of literary characters and allow us to vicariously experience their emotions, thoughts and actions. All these elements – story, structure and a willingness to lay bare difficult themes – may be missing in our conversations with family, friends and our therapists, making it harder for us to connect with them, let alone with ourselves – with the parts of us that went missing. Literature has an uncanny ability to do just this, rescuing us when we are at our most vulnerable, bringing us to shore and reassuring us that we are not alone and that we'll always be supported.

I recommended that in addition to reading, Tatyana should journal and reflect on the feelings and observations that emerged.

LITERARY JOURNALING

Tatyana found literary journaling (see pages 56–60) to be profoundly cathartic. In her journal, she wrote:

The diagnosis feels like a bomb has exploded in my face. So many emotions. Denial, disbelief, shock, anger, fear, sadness – [they] brought significant pain, occupying different parts of me in different spaces of time. I am still processing it all, it leaves me overwhelmed and drained. As I find my feet, I am having to think about what I'll tell the others. The anxiety of telling people. I saw how easily Paul Kalanithi confided in his friends and family in *When Breath Becomes Air*, seeing them as allies, and I want to find this confidence, this courage and this faith in other people. That they are there to help me. I have drawn out a list of things I would like other people to know as a way of managing both my anxiety and expectations of others:

- Please bear with me, I am trying to reconcile myself into this new identity.
- Please reach out – it makes me feel connected.
- Please don't ignore my new state – it would be painful. I am going through a lot and need that to be acknowledged.
- Please don't take it personally if I come across as 'off' with you – it's not you or something you said. I am living through hell.

- Please share your happy/good news. I'd still like to enjoy/ celebrate your happiness.
- Be kind always. We never know what someone else is going through.

Dying so young, I could feel Kalanithi's soul. The agony he felt of not fulfilling unrealised ambitions as a successful neurosurgeon rang true for me. There's so much I would like to do with my life, to achieve, to celebrate, to share with family and friends.

What offered hope is that Kalanithi was exploring what would give his life meaning, with the little time he had left. And the same question is helping me think more clearly. I found comfort in Graham Greene's words: that life was lived in the first twenty years and the remainder was just reflection.

Kalanithi eloquently puts it:

Everyone succumbs to finitude. I am not the only one who reaches this pluperfect state. Most ambitions are either achieved or abandoned; either way, they belong to the past. The future, instead of the ladder toward the goals of life, flattens out into a perpetual present. Money, status, all the vanities the preacher of Ecclesiastes described hold so little interest: a chasing after wind indeed.

In her journal entries, Tatyana considered how much the experiences of the authors she was reading resonated with her own cancer journey. The dual polarities of 'I can't go on' and 'I absolutely must go on', along with the sense that nothing had changed and yet everything had changed, perfectly encapsulated her own experience. Tatyana would often find herself returning to Paul Kalanithi's memoir when she was feeling low. It persuaded her out of the temporary moments of sadness, knowing that other people had walked this difficult path. In these moments, she was reminded of the unfairness of life and how little of life was in your control.

Perhaps it was about surrendering and letting go – both of expectations and of the fear of the unknown. The need to constantly control every micro-outcome was suffocating. Surrender was liberating. Inspired by Louise Hay's *You Can Heal Your Life*, Tatyana decided to incorporate a deep-breathing exercise from the book titled 'Letting Go' into her daily routine. It involved inhaling and exhaling, inviting relaxation into her scalp, face and forehead, then moving on to her tongue, throat and shoulders, before approaching the back, abdomen and pelvis, and finishing with the legs and feet. This released tension from her body while leaving her feeling incredibly peaceful. Tatyana also harnessed the power of positive affirmations by repeating Hay's words to herself: 'I am willing to let go. I release. I let go. I release all tension. I release all fear. I release all anger. I release all guilt. I release all sadness. I let go of all old limitations. I let go, and I am at peace. I am at peace with myself. I am at peace with the process of life. I am safe.'

A combination of calming techniques and Hay's relatable story encouraged Tatyana to reclaim her inner power. The breathwork forced her to focus on the present and reduce the impact of the despairing thoughts inside her.

As Tatyana was an avid reader, I also suggested that she try Will Schwalbe's *The End of Your Life Book Club*, about a mother–son book club. The titular mother, Mary Anne Schwalbe, was diagnosed with incurable pancreatic cancer at seventy-three, so she spent her last days with her son, immersed in all the books she had always wanted to read. Inspired, Tatyana created her own book club with her mother and sister so that she could enjoy time with the people she loved most doing the thing she loved most. This led to engaging and intimate discussions. Tatyana felt especially alive and present in those moments.

VISUALISING ALTERNATIVE FUTURES

Tatyana's relationship with Aleksei continued to play out in the background. The more I spoke to Tatyana, the more I felt that the relationship was negatively impacting her. The emotionally unavailable partner, like the emotionally unavailable mother, was the one that Tatyana would, of course, feel the most comfortable with.

I asked her to visualise alternative outcomes for the relationship, a visualisation technique that renowned future forecaster Jane McGonigal guides us through as an exercise called 'A Future Scenario' in her book *Imaginable*. McGonigal encourages planning for the future by simulating potential scenarios for situations that we find difficult to navigate. We can mentally time-travel into the future in order to vividly imagine alternative endings through what she refers to as 'specificity training'. This involves focusing on specific details when envisioning our scenarios, so we need to make sure that we build in all five senses (sight, hearing, taste, touch and smell). In carrying out these simulations in our minds, we can begin to feel more hopeful, as we're given the opportunity to experiment with alternative solutions to our problems. Taking an active role in modelling our own futures can reduce the sense of powerlessness we feel, build resilience and offer a renewed sense of agency to pursue what's most important to us.

VISUALISING ALTERNATIVE FUTURES – HOW IT WORKS

Visualising alternative futures or outcomes is exactly what it sounds like: it involves imagining alternative future endings or outcomes for a given situation, no matter how impossible they seem at first. This is a conventional visualisation technique that can be used in any form of therapy or coaching, and is not a 'bibliotherapy' technique.

This technique was inspired by Jane McGonigal, a futurist at the Institute of the Future. She discusses a variety of techniques for creating an optimal future for yourself in her book *Imaginable*.

Imagining alternative endings is an excellent way to problem-solve as well as motivate ourselves to create a future that we desire. It increases both hope and empathy, as we learn to acknowledge our needs and act in ways that will allow ourselves to meet these needs. It encourages us to feel the emotions we might need to feel in order to move past a painful event or episode. This form of practising self-compassion and self-care can truly be life-changing, inspiring and empowering, and is scientifically proven to build hope pathways in the brain.

During my third session with Tatyana, I asked her to imagine alternative outcomes to her existing relationship. I wanted her to recognise that it was within her power to make a change if she was unhappy. At first, she seemed stuck in the past, unable to visualise any alternative future or relationship. She could not carry out the mental time travel required. This is often the case for people who have struggled with post-traumatic stress disorder (PTSD).

When it comes to PTSD, the ability to retrieve specific memories from one's past (autobiographical memory) is important for visualising one's future. This is because simulating possible future events depends on much of the same brain processes as remembering past events.[35] For example, if someone is planning a vacation to a new city, they can draw on their past experiences of travelling to similar cities in order to construct a mental image of what the trip might be like. This mental simulation can help individuals anticipate potential challenges and opportunities, and plan accordingly.

In addition, the ability to retrieve specific memories from one's past is also important for developing a sense of identity and personal continuity. People with stronger autobiographical memory abilities are better able to connect their past experiences with their present and future selves, which can lead to a greater sense of coherence and purpose in life.

However, PTSD sufferers, instead of relying on autobiographical memory, tend to rely on an 'overgeneral' memory.

For example, a person with an 'overgeneral' memory might recall a negative experience of failing a test, but they would not be able to remember the details of the experience, such as what the test was about, where and when they took it, or what they did to prepare for it. Instead, they may generalise the experience and conclude that they are not good at taking tests. In contrast, a person with a specific memory would be able to recall the details of the experience, including what happened before and after the test, how they felt at the time, and what they learned from the experience. They may acknowledge that they struggled with that particular test, but they would not generalise the experience to *all* tests. Instead, they would focus on improving their preparation and performance for future tests.

According to a 2014 study in the *Journal of Clinical Psychological Science*, the tendency to rely on overgeneral memory impairs any ability to visualise specific future thinking.[36] A person with an overgeneral memory may struggle to form a sense of self in the future, and may also find it hard to plan for the future and set goals. However, the good news is that by processing the trauma from past memories, it can become easier to repair the cognitive functions of problem-solving, imagining future outcomes and goal-setting.[37]

Depression, linked to trauma, is also associated with difficulties in retrieving specific past memories,[38] making this process of mental time travel into the future difficult, and Tatyana had struggled with depression all her life.

I gave her time and suggested the following strategies to help improve her memory-retrieval abilities in order to better visualise future events.

- Remembering specific details about a past event, such as what you were wearing, who you were with, and what you were feeling at the time, can help you strengthen your memory-retrieval abilities and make it easier to access past memories in the future.
- Writing about past experiences in a journal can also help you to access memories and use them to construct a mental simulation of a possible future event.

- Mindfulness practices, such as meditation and deep-breathing exercises, can help you access memories. By focusing on the present moment and becoming more aware of your thoughts and emotions, you may be better able to access memories and use them to construct a mental simulation of a possible future event.

Tatyana mentioned a passage she'd read in John Green's *The Fault in Our Stars* that had been reassuring in a bittersweet way.

There will come a time when all of us are dead. All of us. There will come a time when there are no human beings remaining to remember that anyone ever existed or that our species ever did anything. There will be no one left to remember Aristotle or Cleopatra, let alone you. Everything that we did and built and wrote and thought and discovered will be forgotten and all of this will have been for naught. Maybe that time is coming soon and maybe it is millions of years away, but even if we survive the collapse of our sun, we will not survive forever. There was time before organisms experienced consciousness, and there will be time after. And if the inevitability of human oblivion worries you, I encourage you to ignore it. God knows that's what everyone else does.

Listening to this passage, something came over me and I began to cry. I realised I was grieving for Tatyana, as she could not do this for herself. She had never been taught to express sadness. It was repressed, and an emotion her family never displayed, especially her grandparents in St Petersburg, whom she remembered as loving but stern.

As I cried, she began to cry. We held each other's hands and let the sadness and pain flow. This was exactly what was needed in that moment. I asked her to practise the alternative futures at home so that we could discuss her different scenarios at our next session.

During our fourth and final session, Tatyana could see with clarity.

'I've decided to break up with Aleksei.' She smiled. 'I want to use the time I have left to explore new people, new experiences, new lives. I want to live life on steroids – literally and mentally.'

Perhaps she had been persuaded by the books she had read, or perhaps it was the prospect of meeting someone new, of feeling the giddy, light-headedness of a fresh relationship. Tatyana felt hopeful, and sometimes that's all we need to overcome the loss we feel. She realised that she had to live her life to the fullest, and that *now* was the time to pursue everything that was meaningful and important. While death might be the ultimate ending, the concept of death is what allows us to lead a fuller, richer life.

The more Tatyana read about the experiences of others, the more her anxiety melted away. She drew strength from reading stories about people who made peace with the inevitability of death, and this allowed her to reject fear and embrace acceptance. Death is a chapter in all our stories. We may not know how long our book will be, but that's why it's so important to make each chapter count. After all, if you can face death, you can face life.

As Andre Dubus II wrote in *Broken Vessels*: 'We receive and we lose, and we must try to achieve gratitude, and with that gratitude to embrace with whole hearts whatever of life that remains after the losses.'

The theme in the final session seemed to be one of rediscovering hope in all its varieties, despite the finitude of life. Sometimes, bibliotherapy does that: it generates hope through books. Often, the thought of being a hope merchant keeps me doing what I do every day: shining a light in the darker corners of night.

Bibliotherapy Toolkit

Bibliotherapy technique used: Literary journaling.

Recommended for: Self-exploration, self-awareness and processing emotion.

Complementary therapeutic technique used: Visualising alternative futures.

Recommended for: Feeling empowered, motivated and finding a sense of control and inner power.

Books prescribed: Paul Kalanithi's *When Breath Becomes Air*, Audre Lorde's *The Cancer Journals*, Louise Hay's *You Can Heal Your Life*, Will Schwalbe's *The End of Your Life Book Club*, John Green's *The Fault in Our Stars*

BIBLIOTHERAPY TECHNIQUE APPLIED – KEY TAKEAWAYS & EXERCISE

See 'Literary Journaling – Key Takeaways' on page 82, along with the exercise on page 83.

COMPLEMENTARY THERAPEUTIC TECHNIQUE APPLIED – KEY TAKEAWAYS & EXERCISE

Visualising Alternative Futures – Key Takeaways

- Imagine alternative future endings or outcomes for a given situation, regardless of how impossible they might seem at first.
- This is a conventional visualisation technique inspired by Jane McGonigal, a futurist at the Institute of the Future and author of *Imaginable*.
- This practice enables problem-solving behaviour as well as self-motivation.
- It increases hope by building hope pathways in the brain.

Exercise

- Imagine you are going to the park.
- What time is it? Is it day or night?
- Are you alone, or are you there with a friend or someone special to you?
- What are you wearing?
- How are you feeling? As you imagine this, give yourself space to fully express and 'experience' these feelings in the moment, no matter how negative or positive.

- What can you see or hear?
- What can you smell or touch?
- Are you eating something? What does it taste like?
- What's the weather like?
- Now you have warmed up, think about an issue in your life you are struggling to address. If you could magically change it (no matter how impossible that seems) what would you do? What would you hope for? What would the scene look like? How would you be feeling? Try to bring in as much vivid detail as possible.

If you're still struggling with your imagination, then practise remembering positive memories. Think of the time of day it was, what you were doing, who you were with, how you were feeling, what you were eating, smelling, touching. Engage all five of your senses.

Practice makes perfect. The more you practise visualisation techniques, the more focused and aligned to your goals you will feel. You'll experience a sense of agency and the power to change the things that are not working.

5

TESSA

'Be a full person. Motherhood is a glorious gift, but
do not define yourself solely by motherhood. Be a full
person. Your child will benefit from that.'

CHIMAMANDA NGOZI ADICHIE

'Birth is not merely that which divides women from
men: it also divides women from themselves, so that
a woman's understanding of what it is to exist is
profoundly changed. Another person has existed in her,
and after their birth they live within the jurisdiction of
her consciousness. When she is with them, she is not
herself; when she is without them, she is not herself;
and so, it is as difficult to leave your children as it is to
stay with them. To discover this is to feel that your life
has become irretrievably mired in conflict or caught in
some mythic snare in which you will perpetually, vainly
struggle.'

RACHEL CUSK

Client notes: Tessa S. is a former lawyer who wants to redis-cover herself post-motherhood. She craves another identity beyond mum and wife. Tessa feels trapped, and needs meaning and purpose in life again. Slight anxiety. Enjoys memoir, biog-raphy and Russian classics/novels.

When clients remind me of myself, I often have to stop myself from jumping in and providing advice and guidance that's founded on my own experience, as I have not really walked in their shoes or lived the childhood they lived. Our realities must be worlds apart. Despite this, it can still be tempting to draw links between your lived experiences.

Tessa, like me, left the corporate world after having her first baby, Eva. She was nine months into motherhood and struggling to recon-cile her old life with her new one. It was as though a transformation had taken place overnight. She was no longer a woman who contained multitudes, but the mother, the wife, the daughter, the sister, the granddaughter and the friend. Her role was *relational*. She felt that she didn't exist in her own right, and a terrible loneliness settled in. She longed to work again but in a more creative space than the world of corporate law. What she really wanted was a job that would give meaning and purpose that would allow her to connect with the more artistic parts of herself that she had neglected.

Tessa's desire to balance motherhood with work is something that women have struggled with throughout history. In Julia Baird's biog-raphy *Victoria: The Queen*, she references letters and diary entries that highlight the Queen's frustrations with being held hostage to child-rearing. She called this the *Schattenseite* or 'shadow side' of marriage.

The following extract is from a letter Victoria wrote to her Uncle Leopold in response to his wish for her to have a large and happy family, as referenced in Baird's biography:

I think, dearest Uncle, you cannot *really* wish me to be the 'Mamma *d'une nombreuse famille*,' for I think you will see with me the great inconvenience a *large* family would be to us all, and particularly to the country, independent of the hardship and inconvenience to myself; men never think, at least seldom think, what a hard task it is for us women to go through this *very often*.

Another extract referenced by Baird is from Victoria's diary:

Aches—and sufferings and miseries and plagues—which you must struggle against—and enjoyments etc. to give up—constant precautions to take, you will feel the yoke of a married woman ... I had 9 times for eight months to bear with those above-named enemies and I own it tired me sorely; one feels so pinned down— one's wings clipped—in fact, at the best ... only half oneself— particularly the first and second time. This I call the 'shadow side' as much as being torn away from one's loved home, parents and brothers and sisters. And therefore, I think our sex a most unenviable one.

While we have made huge strides over the past century when it comes to attitudes towards women and creating a more egalitarian society, the lives of women post-motherhood can still feel limiting and circular. Many women struggle with the idea that it's okay to do what makes you happy, even if that doesn't fit neatly with the expectations of the people around you.

This is something I have recognised in many of my female clients. One of four siblings, Tessa had grown up in Somerset and now lived in Hamburg with her German spouse. Her own mother had been faced with the same dilemma decades earlier. After giving birth to her first child, Edward, Tessa's mother had struggled over whether she should return to work. In the end, she stayed at home until Tessa, who was the youngest, was four, and ultimately managed to strike a happy medium by working part-time at the local council. However, Tessa would often watch as her mother chastised her father for assuming that it was her responsibility to do the lion's share of domestic work simply because she was a woman. Tessa remembered being irritated at the time, as she felt her mother was constantly complaining. Now, looking back, she understands. She has become her mother. She recognises her mother's struggle to find a way out, to step up, to ask for what she needed. For far too long, it had been easier to take care of everyone else's needs before her own.

It sounded like Tessa's mother had strived to find a balance between motherhood and part-time work; however, without any family support, she felt powerless. She was constantly spinning plates, and any one of them could fall at any time.

Now, Tessa was experiencing a similar sense of lacking agency. She felt her mother had devoted her life to Tessa and her siblings, and she had to do the same. Her blind spot was her inability to see that she did have agency, and that it was possible to seek external support in order to pursue her professional dreams.

Tessa knew what she wanted: a new career as an interior designer. Her future path had been something she'd agonised over for a long time before she finally took the plunge and quit her job. The decision had been stressful for her, but decisions are like plasters waiting to be removed. Once you pull off the plaster, you might be pleasantly surprised with how well the wound has healed. Once you make a decision, you can often find the peace and clarity that had evaded you.

Every one of us has the freedom to take charge and do things at will, which I try to reiterate as much as possible to my clients. Freedom means taking responsibility for our actions and choices. This can be frightening. Having complete control can feel unfamiliar and overwhelming, especially if you're not used to it. It's easier to blame external factors for our problems and misgivings. It's also easier to be submissive. We hold on tight to the false belief that changing the things around us will be what makes all the difference. But often, this is not the case. Deep down, Tessa believed she had limited agency. She did not feel she had the power to change things – to ask her husband to work with her to find a childcare solution that might enable her to work. There was a sense of inertia, and Tessa was holding on to it. Tessa's mother had given up work to look after Tessa and her siblings, and now she was following the same pattern, an inherited sense of powerlessness holding them both hostage. I wanted Tessa to see she had more agency than she believed she was capable of.

LITERARY REFLECTIVE PRACTICE USING NOVEL AND MEMOIR THERAPY

To help Tessa feel more hopeful and empowered, I suggested a bibliotherapy technique I refer to as a literary reflective practice using novel and memoir therapy.

LITERARY REFLECTIVE PRACTICE USING NOVEL AND MEMOIR THERAPY – HOW IT WORKS

'The novel is sogged with humanity'

E. M. FORSTER

Literary reflective practice using novels and memoirs follows the Literary Reflective Practice Framework outlined on page 74.

The novel form was popularised in the nineteenth century and captured the cultures and attitudes of the time, exploring people's social, emotional and cognitive capacities through characters in a way literature had never done before. It examined people's interior and exterior lives, diving into their true selves and their false selves, and inviting ways of looking at life that may or may not have been conventional, offering in-depth vistas into an author's mind. Fiction allows for the greatest expressions of human life, often ones that we would be too scared or overwhelmed to explore in real life. Novels offer escapism and perspective, and enable us to access both our conscious and unconscious minds from a distance – from a safe space.

A safe space is key. Feeling safe allows us to let our guards down (or relax our 'defences') and begin to explore feelings that we may have been avoiding, perhaps because they are too painful, or perhaps because it's hard to access them or pinpoint what exactly we are feeling. As we reflect and observe, sometimes we can connect to these feelings and process them ourselves by expressing them through the written or spoken word. We may find we can discover insights and explore coping strategies through the literature. At other times, we may need the help of a counsellor or therapist to work through these thoughts and observations.

Memoir behaves similarly with its exploration of the character and self. And working with both forms, like regular therapy, can reset our mental space, giving us distance and time to reconsider our present lives. Someone once said that reading a novel or memoir was like taking a 'hit of a narrative drug', and I could not agree more.

Through the use of characters, emotion and language, novels and memoirs enable the reader to empathise with and relate to the protagonist(s). By examining the experiences of fictional or unknown characters, readers activate similar neural pathways to those they would when experiencing real-life situations, through third-person theory of

mind.[39,]* According to a 2013 study, literary fiction specifically can improve theory of mind because of the narrative
being character-driven rather than plot-driven and focusing on a character's innermost thoughts and feelings,
triggering these theory of mind processes through
simulation and, as a result, empathy.[40] Memoirs follow a
similar character-driven narrative, giving us access to the
memoirist's innermost thoughts and feelings.

And so, a male reader in the West can suddenly relate
to a female teenager in India, or a Scandinavian native can
empathise with a member of the Māori tribe by reading
Māori novels (Keri Hulme's prize-winning *The Bone People*
comes to mind as an excellent example).

To get Tessa started on this reflective practice, I recommended Rachel
Cusk's *A Life's Work*, as it explores the complexity of motherhood

---

* The third-person theory of mind is a cognitive ability to understand that other
people have beliefs, desires, intentions and emotions that are separate from one's
own. This means that an individual with a third-person theory of mind can recognise that other people have their own perspectives, thoughts and feelings, and can
use this understanding to predict and explain their behaviour. This ability typically
develops during early childhood and is considered an essential component of social
cognition. It enables individuals to navigate complex social interactions and form
meaningful relationships with others. The term 'third-person theory of mind' has
been used to describe the ability to understand the mental states of others from an
objective perspective.
The concept of theory of mind was first introduced by the British psychologists
David Premack and Guy Woodruff in 1978. They used the term to describe the
cognitive ability of chimpanzees to understand the intentions and beliefs of other
chimpanzees. Since then, the concept has been expanded to include human development and social cognition.

without judgement, and I hoped it would offer Tessa a space to explore and honour her own conflicting feelings. To encourage Tessa to assert herself more, I also suggested that she read Rana El Kaliouby's *Girl Decoded*, a memoir about El Kaliouby's goal to pioneer the world's first emotional intelligence technology that would capture the 'unseen emotions' in voice, body language and facial expressions that are often lost over text. In pursuit of her dream, she gave up everything she knew in Egypt – including her husband, her family and a cultural community – and settled in Boston, where she was better equipped to make her dream a vision. A story of transformation but also one of personal power and pursuit, it shows that sometimes we have to challenge ourselves to take the path less travelled in order to find greater joy and fulfilment. Reading fictional or real-life stories of personal transformation encourages us to reconsider our own pain and illuminates possible paths that we can take to heal and embrace transformation. And the path we take does not need to be as extreme as El Kaliouby's one – we all have our own boundaries and limits. The key is that we focus on our inner power and agency to make the changes we need to make for ourselves, so that our own needs and goals can be met.

There is no fixed version of the self. Our personalities are modular and adaptable; different people and situations bring out different sides of us. But Tessa felt she was stuck in a box labelled 'mother and wife', and so she was desperate to access the other parts of her that were seemingly locked away. She wanted to show the world that, yes, she was a mother, and, yes, she was a wife, but that she also existed beyond both of those roles. She wanted the people around her to know that she was so much more – she wanted to be seen for who she truly was.

*

As part of my approach to novel and memoir therapy, I asked Tessa to engage in a literary reflective practice with the memoirs that I had suggested. As she read the passages, I wanted her to keep three questions in mind:

- What feelings were coming up for her as she read and reflected? What was the significance of the emotions that were aroused?
- Were there any passages or moments in the text that particularly resonated with her? Why did they resonate?
- With the awareness she had gained, what was the best path for her to move forward? What were her goals and what were the next steps in making them happen?

Tessa came to the next session with her notes from this exercise, and I was curious to read about what she had discovered through this process. She mentioned that she had found herself drawn to Elena Ferrante's *The Lost Daughter*, the story of a middle-aged, divorced English professor who has an estranged relationship with her daughters after pursuing her professional career and engaging in an affair as a young mother, leaving the care of her daughters to her ex-husband and remaining largely absent. Tess had also included notes from this. She wrote:

When Ferrante states that 'the hardest things to talk about are the ones that we ourselves can't understand', I could totally resonate with these words. My own ambivalence, like Leda's, began to ring true. Initially, it starts as an annoyance and then you realise that it is groundhog day, day in, day out. Literally looking for a break – and then when a break comes, like Cusk states in *A Life's Work*: 'The prospect is exciting, for it is when the baby sleeps that I liaise, as if it were a lover, with my former life. These liaisons, though always thrilling, are often frantic. I dash about the house unable to decide what to do: to read, to work, to telephone my friends.'

Then it became clear this was going to be for life. It had never occurred to me the weight of the responsibility I was taking on until I was in it. No matter how much people warn you what it will be like when you have children – a lifelong commitment, there's no escape – you don't fully realise what this means. Annoyance turns into despair and then into dread, knowing that tomorrow will bring the same burden of domestic life. To me, this is how I read Ferrante's words in those initial pages – an inability to fathom what we are currently feeling and why we are feeling so negative, when motherhood is meant to be this joyous event that's filled with love.

Of course, I love being a mother and my children are so incredibly precious to me, but no one tells you how much of yourself you are giving up. Especially of the previous lives and identities you have known. Having children is one of the biggest life-changing identity-shakers out there, and it takes a while for that to sink in. Both *The Lost Daughter* and *A Life's Work* have shown me that it's okay to feel both love and frustration.

Unfortunately, mothers do not receive enough support, and this is where the conflict between motherhood and 'careerhood' arises – as women, we're made to choose, to feel like we're allowed one or the other. As Cusk writes in *A Life's Work*: 'But the issue of children and who looks after them has become, in my view, profoundly political, and so it would be a contradiction to write a book about motherhood without explaining to some degree how I found the time to write it. For the first six months of Albertine's life, I looked after her at home while my partner continued to work. This experience forcefully revealed to me something to which I had never given much thought: the fact that after a child is born the lives of its mother and father diverge, so that where before they were living in a state of some equality, now they exist in a sort of feudal relation to each other. A day spent at home caring for a child could not be more different from a day spent working in an office. Whatever their relative merits, they are days spent on opposite sides of the world.' Cusk's words encapsulated everything I had been feeling. In being able to acknowledge this, I feel free to move forward. I believe I can transform these feelings into something more positive for the future.

A few weeks later, once we had finished our sessions, Tessa emailed that she had found Rana El Kaliouby's story in *Girl Decoded* inspirational, and while she didn't intend to traverse oceans and begin a new life elsewhere, she wanted to revisit a project close to her heart: opening her own interior design consultancy. She had even pulled together a business plan and applied for financing. She mentioned that in a couple of months, Eva would be starting nursery three days a week, and this would give her more time to spend developing the business.

On reading this, I smiled. For the first time, Tessa was taking charge. She was finally feeling confident again. I was surprised to learn she had made an application to the bank. She was thinking ahead and had already built in a plan for childcare too. She hadn't had a chance to read Julia Baird's *Victoria: The Queen* yet, but it was next on her list.

Bibliotherapists spend their lives rummaging through libraries, bookstores, other people's bookshelves, even university archives and museum collections, all in the hope that they can offer readers access to new worlds, spaces, thoughts, people and feelings. Think of us as personalised literary search engines. Sometimes the works we recommend push emotional buttons, trigger nostalgic memories and facilitate leaps of imagination. This is the power of reading.

Tessa leveraged this power, and it allowed her to make remarkable progress. She went from uncertainty to conviction, and it allowed her to settle on a future path. I wondered if she would see me again.

Twenty-five weeks later, Tessa launched her own interior design consultancy. She sent me a thoughtful email thanking me for the recommendations and insights, and also invited me to her launch party in London. She was gracious and appreciative. I was touched by her kind words, and upon reading them, I felt this was my – as Virginia Woolf so aptly put it – 'moment of vision': a reminder of why I do the work I do, and a sign that bibliotherapy is slowly but surely working its magic.

Bibliotherapy Toolkit

Bibliotherapy techniques used: Literary reflective practice using novel and memoir therapy.

Recommended for: Empathy and self-understanding, processing feelings of helplessness and powerlessness, finding your voice and inner power (agency) and feeling seen.

Books prescribed: Rachel Cusk's *A Life's Work*, Elena Ferrante's *The Lost Daughter,* Rana El Kaliouby's *Girl Decoded*, Julia Baird's *Victoria: The Queen.*

BIBLIOTHERAPY TECHNIQUES APPLIED – KEY TAKEAWAYS & EXERCISES

Literary Reflective Practice Using Novel and Memoir Therapy – Key Takeaways

- Novels and memoirs behave similarly, offering a space for readers to connect and resonate with the feelings of the characters or memoirist.
- *See 'Literary Reflective Practice Framework' on page 74.*

Exercise

1. Reflect on a passage, page or sentence that has specific resonance.
   What was it about this page, passage or sentence that connected with you?

2. How did it make you feel?
   What feelings came up for you? If you're struggling with labelling the feeling, this list might help, inspired by Brené Brown's Atlas of the Heart:

- **Challenging or painful emotions:** stress, overwhelm, anxiety, worry, excitement, dread, fear, vulnerability, anger, self-righteousness, heartbreak, betrayal, hurt, disconnection, feeling invisible, loneliness, shame, guilt, humiliation, embarrassment, anguish, despair, sadness, hopelessness, grief, envy, jealousy, resentment, boredom, disappointment, regret, frustration, confusion.
- **Positive emotions:** joy, happiness, calm, contentment, gratitude, relief, tranquillity, love, trust, belonging, connection, compassion, empathy, hope, admiration, awe, wonder, curiosity, surprise, yearning, nostalgia, amusement.

3. What meanings do you draw from your feelings?
   What would you like to share about this experience with someone close to you? Upon reflection, what lessons can you draw from this experience? This should bring a sense of conclusion and closure on anything that's bothering you. Remember to be self-compassionate and/or to practise self-forgiveness. Equally, it's important to forgive others for hurts in the past so that you can move forward.

4. With the awareness and understanding you have gained, how would you like to move forward?
   This could be a new way of looking at things. New perspectives bring different ways of being and new outlooks. It could be that you set new goals or make new resolutions. It could even be saying no to someone or something, drawing stronger boundaries or taking some time out to think. Whatever it is, this exercise should help bring clarity and focus, especially when we are feeling overwhelmed, confused, powerless or indecisive.

6

ANNETTE AND DAVID

'Love enjoys knowing everything about you; desire needs mystery. Love likes to shrink the distance that exists between me and you, while desire is energised by it. If intimacy grows through repetition and familiarity, eroticism is numbed by repetition.'

ESTHER PEREL, *MATING IN CAPTIVITY*

Client notes: Annette and David are seeking reconnection and romance through literature so that they can focus on being a couple again.

Annette and David's story is not uncommon. The birth of three kids in quick succession had completely changed their relationship, and with three young boys now aged seven, five and three, domesticity and practicality had got in the way of intimacy, excitement and desire.

It was almost impossible to find time for romance. But as renowned couples therapist Esther Perel writes in *Mating in Captivity*:

> for [erotically intelligent couples], love is a vessel that contains both security and adventure, and commitment offers one of the great luxuries of life: time. Marriage is not the end of romance, it is the beginning. They know that they have years in which to deepen their connection, to experiment, to regress, and even to fail. They see their relationship as something alive and ongoing, not a *fait accompli*. It's a story that they are writing together, one with many chapters, and neither partner knows how it will end. There's always a place they haven't gone yet, always something about the other still to be discovered.

Commitment should not mark the end of excitement and passion; instead, it should be the start of a fascinating journey together, where we are willing to take risks to discover parts of each other we have never known or to experiment in new ways, constantly reinventing ourselves and the relationship, to keep novelty and wonder alive, and to avoid the stagnancy that the routine of domesticity brings.

Annette and David had come to see me as they wanted to rekindle the romantic spark in their marriage through literature. The goal of our sessions was to find ways for them to reconnect with the feelings they might have experienced at the start of their relationship, so that they could remember why they fell in love with each other in the first place. When you're first getting to know someone, it's exciting; suddenly, a future filled with endless possibilities opens up, and there is also the naive promise of wholeness, of oneness. However, with time, we discover that perfection in a relationship isn't possible – nor is it desirable. No couple is perfect. There will always be differences that we live with, that we embrace – and that's what true love is. If we try to combine the giddiness and affection at the start of a relationship with the loyalty and commitment that only develop over time, we can nourish and recharge our connection with our partner.

David and Annette were childhood sweethearts who had met in secondary school. Originally from Normandy in France, Annette had moved to north London with her parents and had met David while studying for her A levels. They had both chosen English A level, and often found themselves discussing homework after class. David lived five minutes away from Annette, so he would often walk her home after school. There had been this undeniable chemistry between them. For David, he remembered not being able to take his eyes off Annette in those first few months of getting to know each other. Annette had found David incredibly attractive, easy to talk to and kind. The relationship began as a platonic one, but it wasn't long before it transformed into a romantic one. They would spend most weekends together studying at each other's houses, playing badminton with friends or going to the cinema on a Saturday night.

David went on to pursue law at university in the Midlands while Annette decided to become a teacher and complete her training in London. Their relationship became a long-distance one for a while, but they spent as many weekends as possible together during the three years that David was away. It was hard at times, but they made it work. David secured a training contract at a small law firm in London, and they moved in together in a spacious, two-bedroom flat in north London, not far from both sets of parents. Annette found a teaching post at a local state school.

Life was good, and while they had their ups and downs like any other couple, they had settled into a routine. Marriage had not always been on the cards – neither of them had strong feelings about it. Their desire for children and a wish to eventually start a family led them to tie the knot in a small, beautiful ceremony in Brittany after twelve years of being together. Ironically, though, once they had children, their relationship started to falter.

Family life, especially with young children, can often feel routine and repetitive, making us all the more nostalgic for the excitement, fun and unpredictability that a blossoming relationship offers. When we reach crisis point, though, we must learn to rediscover ourselves and each other again, even amidst the frenzy of caring for others. This journey back to ourselves brings newness and excitement, while also allowing us to revisit memories of how things used to be. Ultimately, it's not about changing ourselves, but inviting our partner to see us with new eyes. As Proust wrote, 'The real voyage of discovery consists not in seeking new landscapes but in having new eyes.' Annette and David were going to have to explore their relationship from new vantage points and invite change into their very busy lives.

Rather than ruminating on the festering issues, I wanted to focus on how they could feel better together in the *present* moment. Bibliotherapy was a natural fit for them, as they were both voracious readers. I wanted their passion for reading to reunite them as a couple and restore some of the emotional intimacy that was now lacking in their relationship.

DATE-NIGHT BOOK CLUB

As cheesy as it might be, a date-night book club was my key literary prescription. What better way to spend quality time together than by reading side by side and connecting over engaging and animated discussion? This was also my way of disrupting the domestic routine of which they had both grown weary.

My challenge was finding something that they would both enjoy. David was into non-fiction, particularly autobiography and business, as well as travel and nature writing. Some of his favourite books included Walter Isaacson's *Steve Jobs*, Christopher Bell's *Churchill and the Dardanelles* and Robert Macfarlane's *Underland*. Annette, on the other hand, loved literary fiction, as well as fantasy and historical fiction. Hilary Mantel's *Wolf Hall* trilogy was the perfect confluence of her reading tastes. I instinctively reached for memoir. It offers a narrative structure, which would suit Annette, but also offers real-life detail, which would appeal to David. I also kept in mind that both were drawn to history, so we arrived at Bernard D. Brown's *Dear Selma: A World War II Love Letter Romance*. This is an epistolary memoir of Bernard's experiences as a teenager during the Second World War, from training in an army college in Oklahoma to fighting on the frontline in France and Germany, all the while writing letters to his childhood friend Selma. It is a story of war, but also a chronicle of their love, and Bernard's letters perfectly encapsulate how their friendship evolved into romance. There's something about reading the story of a couple falling in love that persuades us to try harder at our own relationships – we find inspiration in their stories, wanting to emulate them. In addition, we're drawn to their experiences so that we can learn how to optimise ours. Coupled with the backdrop of war, we are pulled into a tense space where the sense of danger and uncertainty brings both the readers and the characters closer together.

LETTER-WRITING

The epistolary format was also the perfect precursor to the next piece of homework that I assigned to David and Annette: in between the weekly date-night book clubs, I suggested that they write a letter to each other. I hoped this would inspire a silent goal to keep each other in mind throughout the week, to share compassion and kindness towards each other, and ultimately to share love in their writing. They could even use these letters to state grievances, but also gratitude, affection and appreciation for one another. Through letter-writing, I hoped they could recreate some of the excitement of those thrilling moments when they first fell in love.

Letter-writing is a creative bibliotherapy technique I use for addressing interpersonal or relationship issues due to the emotional intimacy it fosters between reader and writer.

LETTER-WRITING – HOW IT WORKS

Letter-writing is way of presenting oneself to another in a deeply honest way. It took off in the eighteenth century, a time known as 'The Great Age of Letter-Writing'. It was a medium through which you could explore your own thoughts, feelings, ideas and identity. At the same time, you were writing with a reader in mind, inviting them to share in your innermost thoughts. This created a contract of trust between the receiver (the reader) and the sender (the writer).

Letter-writing is a useful therapeutic tool, because it has all the elements of a therapeutic alliance: trust, intimacy, openness, honesty, the sharing of oneself. It gives the receiver space and time to construct an equally thoughtful response without the need to respond straight away (as you would in a conversation or when using modern-day instant messaging), making the response more meaningful and purposeful.

It can also be a useful way to share the things you find hard to express in person; and it can give the recipient the time and space to offer a more considered, thoughtful response. For example, the more emotionally intense 'requests' – such as making a confession, seeking or granting forgiveness, or getting back in touch with someone after an estrangement, argument or betrayal – can trigger various emotions in the recipient. Letters allow us to make these requests or share these feelings without risking the recipient's immediate emotional reaction, which may be negative in the first instance.

In bibliotherapy, letters can be written to another person, to a protagonist in a novel, to the author of a book, or even to our future or past selves. There is no pressure to send your letter if you don't feel ready. Simply the exercise of writing the letter can be therapeutic.

Why Letter-Writing is Beneficial for Couples Bibliotherapy

For couples therapy specifically, letter-writing can improve trust. By taking time to write the letter, we are demonstrating our commitment to the other person and showing that we care. A letter from a significant other can be deeply romantic and bring about feelings of love, excitement, warmth and even desire. The authenticity, intimacy and romance of it can really take us back to the feelings we might have had about the other person when we first fell in love.

Words, after all, connect us and bring us closer, and that is the goal of couples bibliotherapy. Let the letters become your shared vision and affirmation of how you'd like to forge ahead with your life together as a couple.

Letter-writing felt like the perfect way to reinject romance into Annette and David's relationship. It created anticipation, particularly for Annette and David and their upcoming date night. It was something to look forward to.

I wanted to see how they both got on with each exercise over a fortnight before I saw them again, as this would give them time to enjoy two date-night book clubs, and to write and receive a letter twice. I also had a few more suggestions up my sleeve.

LOVE LANGUAGES

The first was to work out their love languages using Gary Chapman's *The 5 Love Languages*. Chapman believes that we experience love in five different ways or 'languages': quality time, words of affirmation, gifts, acts of service, and physical touch. I suggested they work out which ones were the most meaningful for both of them, and to focus on these love languages during their date night. So now they had not one book but two to discuss at their first date night the following Friday.

LITERARY CONVERSATIONS THROUGH TWELVE QUESTIONS

The second thing I asked them to do was to complete a set of twelve literary questions. I get clients to do these together on their very first date-night book club. There is an energy in these questions that can help to reignite dormant passion, as the sharing of self through the responses encourages feelings of closeness and intimacy. These questions have been designed and inspired by a variety of literature on relationships and attachment.

1. What's your favourite book from your childhood? Why?
2. What book should be mandatory reading for everyone?

3.   What book has influenced you the most?

4.   If you could host a literary dinner party, who would you invite and why?

5.   If there is a book you would gift someone you love, what would it be and why?

6.   What's your favourite love story? Why? What draws you to this story?

7.   What are the most interesting books you have read? What makes them so, in your opinion?

8.   What are some of your reading aspirations? A goal to get through a certain fraction of your to-be-read list? A regular book club with your favourite people in the whole world? An opportunity to meet an author you love and pick their brain?

9.   Name a book that you haven't read yet that you are really excited about reading.

10.   Think of a friend who is in a difficult situation right now. What book(s) would you suggest they read?

11.   Are there any hidden gems in your reading life? Little-known books that you wish more people knew about?

12.   What gives your life meaning? (This question is inspired by Viktor Frankl's *Man's Search for Meaning*.)

READING POETRY ALOUD AS A COUPLE

Finally, I suggested something purely experimental. I wanted them to read love poems aloud to each other at some point mid-week, in between the date-night book clubs, in order to keep up the momentum, energy and excitement of the date nights. I asked them to make meaning from it, and to discuss what they found striking. And if they felt inspired, I suggested they could even write each other a poem and then read these out loud. Reading poetry to our loved ones is a deeply romantic act, a bibliotherapy spell for romance.

READING POETRY ALOUD AS A COUPLE – HOW IT WORKS

Reading poetry together can be hugely restorative and create room for connection. It can trigger discussion and help us focus on each other and our goals as a couple.

Poets, through their carefully chosen words, phrases and rhythm, create a particular mood or atmosphere, one that has a calming effect on the mind, slowing us down and focusing both partners on the present. When we read poetry aloud together, we often need to pay closer attention to our breathing in order to maintain the rhythm and flow of the poem. We become more mindful of our breathing patterns, and this can lead to a sense of calm and relaxation.

In addition, the shared experience of engaging in an activity together creates intimacy and connection that reduces feelings of anxiety and stress, which can contribute to slower, more regulated breathing.

Reading poetry aloud together also instils a sense of romance, as poetry's use of language is more expressive and concise, creating vivid and sensory images that can evoke powerful emotions. Love poetry in particular uses rich imagery and metaphor to convey the intensity of romantic feelings.

Novels can also be powerful in instilling a sense of romance, but they may not have the same emotional intensity or concise, expressive language as poems. This makes poetry more effective than novels for restoring romance and togetherness, acting as a beacon of hope that things are heading in the right direction.

When I caught up with them on the phone a few weeks later, these simple habits had brought back some of the romance they had been missing over the last few years, and they felt a renewed sense of connection. They continued the date-night book club and letter-writing, and although the poetry was a unique experience, they decided it wasn't something they would do on a regular basis. Habits were born, and they felt these were sustainable and injected the right amount of romance and intimacy in the midst of a hectic family schedule.

And that's the value of reading and reading together. It gives us the opportunity to find the love languages we need to express how much the other person means to us. Sharing an immersive experience that puts us both on the same page brings us closer, and letting ourselves be positively influenced by other people's stories of love can help us rediscover our own.

Bibliotherapy Toolkit

Bibliotherapy techniques used: Date-night book club, letter-writing, literary conversations through twelve questions, reading poetry aloud as a couple.

Recommended for: Restoring intimacy in a relationship.

Books prescribed: Bernard D. Brown's *Dear Selma: A World War II Love Letter Romance* and Gary Chapman's *5 Love Languages.*

BIBLIOTHERAPY TECHNIQUES APPLIED – KEY TAKEAWAYS & EXERCISES

Letter-Writing – Key Takeaways

- Letter-writing as an intimate form of presenting oneself to another in a deeply honest way.
- It's a medium through which you can explore your thoughts, feelings and ideas.
- As you are sharing your innermost thoughts, this openness and intimacy creates a contract of trust between the receiver and the sender.
- Letter-writing has all the elements of a therapeutic alliance:

trust, intimacy, openness, honesty and the sharing of oneself.

- It makes it easier for the sender to express the thoughts and feelings they may find challenging to do in person.
- It gives the receiver space and time to construct an equally thoughtful response without the pressure to respond straight away, or without risking an impulsive reaction, making the response more meaningful, considered and purposeful.
- These letters can be written to another person, to a protagonist, to an author, or to our future or past selves.
- A letter written does not always have to be sent. The simple act of writing the letter can be therapeutic.

Letter-Writing for Couples Bibliotherapy – Key Takeaways

- A letter can improve trust and bring back past feelings of love, excitement, warmth and desire.
- A series of letters over time can become your shared vision and affirmation of what you'd like your future relationship to look like.

Exercise

Commit to writing to your partner once a week. Be open, honest and authentic in your writing. Handwritten letters are preferable, although emails will still work.

Use the following prompts to guide you:

- Name one or two wonderful ways in which your partner makes you feel loved and accepted.
- Show how much you appreciate each other, what you value the most, what is going really well and what you'd like to see more of.
- Is there a fantasy (romantic or sexual) that you'd like to experience with your partner? Describe it in detail. Where would you like it to take place? Would you want it to be a one-off event or a frequent occurrence? How would you like to feel at the end of it? How could you sustain this feeling?
- How do you currently deal with stress, frustration or disappointment with each other? How would you like to be able to deal with it going forward?
- How can you show each other that you are a unit?
- What is your vision for your relationship going forward (your dreams, goals, aspirations)?

At the end of the week, reflect on these letters together, and perhaps use the following as discussion points:

- What resonated?
- What made you feel closer?
- What came as a surprise?
- How would you like to use these letters to help your relationship going forward?
- Did the letters make you feel hopeful?
- If there have been strong feelings of anger, disappointment or frustration, what could you do together to calm these?

- Was there anything missing from the letters that you wish you had expressed/said to each other?

If you need more therapeutic support, consider discussing these letters in couple's counselling, psychotherapy, bibliotherapy or coaching.

Reading Poetry Aloud as a Couple – Key Takeaways

- Reading poetry together can be restorative and create opportunities for connection.
- It triggers discussion and helps us focus on each other and our goals as a couple.
- A poet's carefully chosen words, phrases and rhythm create a particular mood or atmosphere, calming the mind and focusing both partners on the present.
- When we read poetry aloud together, we pay closer attention to our breathing to maintain the rhythm and flow of the poem. We become mindful of our breathing patterns. This leads to a sense of calm and relaxation.
- The expressive language of poetry, especially love poetry, creates rich sensory images that can evoke powerful emotions.

Exercise
Find a poem that you both connect with and read it aloud together. Some of my favourites include 'This Marriage' by Rumi (see below),

an excerpt from *Captain Corelli's Mandolin* by Louis de Bernières, and 'To Love Is Not to Possess' by James Kavanaugh.

Take it in turns to read aloud, or perhaps assign lines or verses. Focus on your breath and pace, as this exercise is designed to help slow you down so that you can feel more connected. You may even want to light a candle to create a relaxed atmosphere and add to the reading experience.

Discuss each poem using the following prompts:

- How did you both feel after reading this poem?
- Was there any truth in the words?
- Did you connect with it?
- Was there anything about it that made you feel sad?
- Was there anything you could use in your own relationship?
- What takeaways, if any, have you noted from the poem/excerpt/your conversation?

'This Marriage' by Rumi
May these vows and this marriage be blessed.
May it be sweet milk,
this marriage, like wine and halvah.
May this marriage offer fruit and shade
like the date palm.
May this marriage be full of laughter,
our everyday a day in paradise.
May this marriage be a sign of compassion,
a seal of happiness here and hereafter.

May this marriage have a fair face and a good name,
an omen as welcomes the moon in a clear blue sky.
I am out of words to describe
how spirit mingles in this marriage.

7

SAVANNAH

> 'That is part of the beauty of all literature. You discover
> that your longings are universal longings, that you're
> not lonely and isolated from anyone. You belong.'

F. SCOTT FITZGERALD, AS QUOTED IN *BELOVED
INFIDEL* BY SHEILAH GRAHAM AND GEROLD FRANK

*Client notes: Savannah is looking for connection and rep-
resentation. She wants to read characters in fantasy fiction
and young adult fiction that share her own sexuality.*

'I often feel that being asexual is something to be ashamed of,'
Savannah whispered. She looked as though she wanted to disappear
in that moment.

'When did you first discover you were asexual?' I asked, holding
the eye contact. I wanted to simply listen and let her tell her story.

'I remember being twelve years old at the local park with some friends. Everyone was gossiping about who they liked and fancied at school, and for some reason I wasn't remotely interested in swapping notes.'

'And did this absence of feelings continue as you got older?' I asked.

'Yes. I think I realised one day that I just did not care or feel strongly about anyone in the same way that my friends did. It's one of those things: once you hear the word "asexual" and work out what it means, you suddenly notice it everywhere, because a small voice inside your head says, *that's you*! But I've always struggled with the label, so I'm not sure how strong I want this voice to become.'

'That must be quite difficult. To feel that you must hide or silence parts of yourself – especially when it's such a big part of who you are. You're almost asking yourself to be inauthentic, to disconnect from who you are,' I said.

'Exactly, and I am also struggling to see myself represented anywhere. I would love to feel like I'm understood and recognised, and that I'm not alone. If I found a book with an asexual character, I think it would be incredibly affirming. I want to read about *these* people, their struggles, their pain, their experiences.'

Savannah wanted to discover different representations of asexuality in literature. She felt this would validate her own unique experience of asexuality. Asexuality is rare, so it can often feel very lonely if you can't connect with others who identify in the same way – a ready tribe who share your identity and who understand you.

Literature can offer you that connection by introducing you to characters who sympathise with your experience. The first book I suggested to Savannah was Claudie Arsenault's *City of Strife*, the first book in the *City of Spires* trilogy, a political, dystopian fantasy with a LGBTQIAP+ cast that weaves together dynamic relationships and powerful conquests while exploring different sexual identities and orientations. That week, Savannah focused entirely on that one book, caressing it as though she had been given something wholesome, sustaining and nourishing.

The following week during our online session, Savannah mentioned that she felt strangely connected to the world of the book, as if she had found true belonging. Although she had different experiences of sexuality to the protagonists, she felt 'normal' for once, and safe to explore her asexuality through the literature. She felt particularly connected to Cal, who like her was aromantic and asexual.

LETTER-WRITING TO PROTAGONISTS

Given that Savannah had felt a real connection to Cal, I suggested she write a letter to him. I refer to this technique as Letter-Writing to Protagonists.

LETTER-WRITING TO PROTAGONISTS – HOW IT WORKS

Letter-writing to protagonists encourages creativity while allowing the reader (who will be crafting the letters) to feel safe in exposing their true feelings. The reader can

---

cross the threshold into imaginative thinking to prepare a response to the characters that feels natural and establishes a connection.

As cognitive neuroscientist and reading specialist Maryanne Wolf states in *Reader, Come Home: The Reading Brain in a Digital World*, a book that explores the impact of digital technology on our reading habits and the way our brain processes information:

'Letters invite a kind of cerebral pause in which we can think with each other and, if very fortunate, experience a special kind of encounter.'

Expanding on a reader's capacity to hold onto and shift between different perspectives by writing a letter to the protagonist and then writing a response to themselves as if from the protagonist can be very helpful in therapy. In effect, the reader is looking at themselves through the eyes of the protagonist, which can offer a refreshingly new point of view and enhance self-awareness, self-compassion and healing.

Letters assist in externalising a client's problems, as they begin to own the therapeutic process, converting it into a more collaborative effort. This form of correspondence mimics the psychological work of dialogue that is otherwise carried out between two people during traditional therapeutic interventions. This is underpinned by the concept of third-person theory of mind (see page 122): the ability to attribute mental states to other people and see things from other people's perspectives through empathy and creative imagination. It's a skill that's typically developed during early childhood.

In her book *Why We Read Fiction: Theory of Mind and the Novel* Lisa Zunshine illustrates that reading fiction allows us to test and enjoy our theory of mind skills. She writes: 'Our enjoyment of fiction is predicated – at least in part – upon our awareness of our "trying on" mental states potentially available to us but at a given moment differing from our own.'

Maryanne Wolf echoes this sentiment: 'Reading enables us to try on, identify with, and ultimately enter for a brief time the wholly different perspective of another person's consciousness. Through this exposure we learn both the commonality and the uniqueness of our own thoughts.'

It is these complex mental shifts that trigger psychological processes associated with healing.

Note that in this section, we have focused on fiction and writing a letter to the protagonist. For memoirs and other non-fiction, the same technique may be applied by writing to the author or narrator instead.

Savannah wrote Cal a letter acknowledging his experience and, in doing so, she also acknowledged her own. Then she wrote another letter, this time addressed to herself from Cal's perspective, and found the process profoundly cathartic. It was affirming for her to see people like her represented in literature.

In her letter to Cal, she wrote:

Dear Cal,

Upon reading your story, I felt a strong connection to the narrative and the characters. I have always felt like a minority within a minority, with many experiences of rejection and a lack of belonging. Often people assume that people like me and you, who fall into the asexual and aromantic categories, are cold and unfriendly. However, your warmth, sweetness and kindness really shone through. You were always there for your friends throughout, and I felt that the truth about who we are was finally being spoken. I too am loyal to my friends down to a tee. Stay true to yourself, Cal, because through reading about your story, you've taught me to stay true to myself.

Savannah

Here you can see Savannah really empathising with Cal, and extending her compassion because she has been through similar experiences herself, having been misunderstood as cold or uninterested due to her asexuality and aromantic orientation. Savannah refers to Cal and herself as 'we': 'the truth about who we are was finally being spoken'. She recognises her own experiences of being misunderstood in this statement, empathising with her own experience, cultivating an inner compassion and illustrating self-empathy. At the end, she states, 'stay true to yourself, because through reading about your story, you've taught me to stay true to myself' and here we see her embracing and accepting herself, as she is.

Then Savannah switched gears and wrote a response from the perspective of Cal:

Dear Savannah,

Reading your letter brought me joy, like I had made a real differ-ence. I'm super appreciative of you sharing your feelings and thoughts with me, Savannah. It means a lot. We sound like two peas in a pod! I can relate to your experience of often feeling like a minority. The pain of being 'othered' or misunderstood or not truly seen. We're all seeking connection and belonging. And you deserve nothing less. I am glad you felt a sense of belonging upon reading City of Strife.

It's not been an easy journey for me and your astuteness in acknow-ledging the unkindness of some of the other characters in the book has helped me too — by accepting me for who I am. And by reaching out and sharing your experience. I've felt less alone too.

Remember: if you ever feel like you don't belong, think about me and the others out there like us — we are your tribe. Belonging is about being accepted for who you are, rather than having to change yourself so that you can belong.

Yours,

Cal

Here, Savannah has demonstrated her enormous capacity to not only understand and embody the mental state of a fictional character, but also to extend understanding and self-compassion towards herself from the perspective of that character. This multilateral thinking enables self-reflective, self-critical thinking as an adjunct of talk-ing therapy. This is a classic example of how multiple perspectives triggered during reading can encourage a richness of psychological thoughts that can be therapeutic and healing. Savannah had discov-ered an ability to get outside of her own head and into somebody else's mind through the action of reading and writing, ultimately finding herself in the process. Reading can create the beginnings of self-directed therapeutic dialogue and change.

In writing back to herself from the perspective of Cal, Savannah shows how well she understands his character. As she writes back to herself from Cal's perspective, Savannah describes 'the pain of being "othered" or misunderstood or not truly seen'. Here, with newfound perspective, she indirectly acknowledges her own pain, which stems from the challenges of living in a heteronormative society and is able to extend empathy to herself in a compassionate way. Through the simple act of sharing the problem or pain through this imagined correspondence with a protagonist she relates to, Savannah can self-soothe, express and relieve her own pain and feel more at peace with her own reality.

Writing letters in this way is a profound therapeutic process. It reduces the self-exposure that a reader feels, and invites them to share their innermost feelings without the sting of self-consciousness. Savannah's ability to get outside her mind and into Cal's through reading and writing to him led to mental shifts that encouraged more self-expansive thinking. Writing partly to the character and partly to oneself can be validating, ultimately leading to self-acceptance.

This externalising of problems on to paper is the first step towards drawing out the deeply buried traumas of our past. The self-directed therapeutic conversation leads to healing and reparative change. The diverse thinking triggered by shifting mindsets encourages new awareness, different ways of looking at the world that were previously inaccessible. Suddenly, we can see our blind spots, and those of others, too. We are better able to recognise each other's thoughts, desires and beliefs by putting ourselves in the protagonist's shoes and also by reconnecting with parts of ourselves that we have discovered in the protagonist.

During our second session, Savannah reported enjoying two further recommendations I'd made: *The Lady's Guide to Petticoats and Piracy* by Mackenzi Lee and *Loveless* by Alice Oseman.

'I absolutely loved this book. So much attention was paid to making the historical setting realistic and this really added richness to the story. It's also so rare to find a book that focuses on female friendship that doesn't feature an obligatory romantic subplot. It was so refreshing to finally read something that's all about spotlighting the power of platonic relationships and the fulfilment we can derive from working towards a personal goal. For example, Felicity's determination to study medicine despite the odds being stacked against her as a woman in the eighteenth century – reading about her persistence really motivated me to find my own drive. It felt like I'd found in Felicity a kindred spirit and this book felt like one big reminder that I'm asexual and that's okay.'

Savannah also drew great comfort from Alice Oseman's *Loveless*, a young adult novel about a college student called Georgia who discovers that she may identify as asexual and aromantic. The novel explores the complexities of navigating relationships and societal expectations in a world where asexuality is not very well understood.

'It was the book that made me feel I exist. I felt seen and Oseman really nailed the friendship experience for someone like me! Friendships aren't celebrated enough, and sometimes they are better than romantic relationships with partners, yet our culture portrays the romantic relationship as the superior one. It was beautiful. I found a philosophy for friendship and relationships in this book,' Savannah said excitedly.

It was wonderful to see a client so moved by a book. It was a feeling of tremendous satisfaction.

NARRATIVE THERAPY

In the second half of the session, I focused on narrative therapy. Narrative therapy can involve re-authoring or rearranging our own stories to find closure in our personal narratives. It positions us as experts on our own lives. The stories we create often link events and people in chronological order. Strikingly, they tend to mimic a universal storyline of problem, resolution, transformation.

NARRATIVE THERAPY – HOW IT WORKS

'When we have the courage to walk into our story and own it, we get to write the ending.'

BRENÉ BROWN, *DARE TO LEAD*

Narrative therapy has its origins in New Zealand. Developed by therapists Michael White and David Epston, it is a type of psychotherapy that focuses on the stories people tell about their lives and experiences. The goal of narrative therapy is to help individuals understand and reframe their personal narratives in a more positive and empowering way, and to reduce the influence of negative and destructive

---

narratives that may be limiting their potential or causing emotional distress.

In narrative therapy, individuals explore their personal stories, and identify and challenge any negative or oppressive beliefs or patterns that may be embedded within these stories. Through this process of externalising and re-authoring their narratives, individuals can gain greater insight into their own lives, and develop more agency and resilience in dealing with life's challenges.

Some key principles of narrative therapy developed by White and Epston include:

- **Externalising problems:** Narrative therapy encourages individuals to view their problems as external to themselves, rather than as inherent personal flaws. By externalising problems, individuals are better able to gain perspective and distance themselves from negative or limiting beliefs.
- **Deconstructing dominant narratives:** Narrative therapy can challenge dominant cultural narratives or societal expectations that may be contributing to an individual's problems. By deconstructing these narratives, individuals can better understand how they have been influenced by them and how they might be able to construct alternative stories that better align with their own experiences and values.

- **Constructing new narratives:** Narrative therapy can help individuals to create new narratives that are more positive, hopeful and empowering by exploring alternative perspectives, reframing negative experiences in a more positive light, or identifying new ways of viewing oneself and one's life.
- **Acknowledging multiple perspectives:** Narrative therapy recognises that there are often multiple perspectives to any given experience, and encourages individuals to explore and acknowledge these different perspectives. By doing so, individuals can gain a more nuanced understanding of their own experiences and the experiences of others.

Often, it's only in hindsight that we can make sense of our past, accept it and find closure and even hope as we learn to move forward again. If you are in the middle of a difficult story right now, know that this too will pass.

In the book *Discourse, Dialogue and Diversity in Biographical Research: An Ecology of Life and Learning*, Alan Bainbridge, author and senior lecturer in education at Canterbury Christ Church University, explains that the telling of one's life story can make visible something greater, allowing us to transcend time and reconnect with both the past and the future to assist us in working out who we are and what we draw meaning from.

I explained the concept and purpose of narrative therapy to Savannah and encouraged her to give it a go before the session ended. We had a short discussion about it and covered some of her anxieties about her sexual identity and orientation. We also talked about how, over time, she had shifted her perspective from feeling ashamed to embracing her sexual identity, and was feeling excited about life again. After this conversation, she wrote a short narrative about her life that was focused on her asexual orientation and how she is now incredibly proud to be part of that community. Here is an excerpt from her narrative:

I'm tired of living in a world where there is an assumption that long-term, exclusive romantic relationships are the norm. I often used to feel the pressure to date and go out and seek romantic relationships so that one day I could settle down and begin a family. While I'd love to start a family, I'm not sure I really want a romantic or sexual relationship.

Whenever someone spoke about their romantic feelings for me, it made me want to run a mile. It just felt off and my intuition would tell me that something wasn't quite right. And it was about time I listened to my intuition.

Reading books that break the heteronormative mould has been a breath of fresh air, and they have inspired me to create my own LGBQT+ book club to discuss issues of representation.

I'm now twenty-five years old and I've never been in a relationship, kissed someone or had sex. I felt crushed when I was in secondary school at age sixteen, as everyone around me seemed to be having sex, losing their virginity or enjoying their first kisses. I remember people making digs that they tried to pass off as jokes about how I was a loser because I was so inexperienced. I felt ashamed, as though there was something wrong with me, and this was partly because I had never really come across the idea that a lack of sexual or romantic desire was an acceptable norm.

It was only when I began university, and confessed to a friend that I didn't really fancy anyone sexually or romantically that she said, 'I see, so you are asexual then?' She went through all the different sexual identities with me, as well as orientations, and suddenly everything made sense. It was the first time I felt understood. A realisation that there was a name for what I was experiencing, or the way I was, and that it was absolutely acceptable and normal. I didn't feel alone that day because of this. I realised how important my university friendships were to me. They were supportive of who I was. I do feel the world is changing now. There's more acceptance. Books are the first step in educating people [and] giving a platform to people with different sexual identities and orientations [so they can] be heard and seen. [They are also] a therapeutic space for people in the LGBQT+ community.

I've really struggled with accepting myself, it's taken years. It's been a process. But it's only now that my family have come to terms with it, and [that is] further affirmation there's nothing wrong with me. Sometimes, if someone doesn't get it straight away, that's okay too. It's not taking anything away from me. It's none of my business, how they feel about me.

The Alice Oseman book took me back in time to secondary school, those painful times when I felt great anxiety and insecurities about who I was, when I did not have friends I could confide in. In hindsight, though, I do have those friends now. I am grateful. I appreciate this was a journey I needed to go through to embrace what I have now. I can go into the future a lot more supported and aware.

I now bask in the joy that I find in platonic relationships and [know] that a lifelong partnership with someone is possible as long as there are no expectations of it being a romantic or sexual one. Essentially, labels assist in communicating our identity, needs and desires – if they help us assert who we are then that's great, but there's no pressure to use one if you feel that it will put you in a box.

Savannah felt more at peace with her asexuality after reframing her story in this way.

On the days that she feels low or has moments of self-doubt, she rereads her narrative story or the letters between her and Cal to reassure her and help her stay true to herself in a society that is largely heteronormative.

Bibliotherapy Toolkit

Bibliotherapy techniques used: Letters to protagonists, narrative therapy.

Recommended for: Gaining insight into your current situation, finding closure and feeling more empowered.

Books prescribed: Claudie Arsenault's *City of Strife*, Mackenzi Lee's *The Lady's Guide to Petticoats and Piracy*, Alice Oseman's *Loveless*.

BIBLIOTHERAPY TECHNIQUES APPLIED – KEY TAKEAWAYS & EXERCISES

Letter-Writing to Protagonists – Key Takeaways

- This involves the reader preparing a written response to a character that explores a feeling, observation or theme triggered by the text or narrative.
- Letter-writing helps to externalise a client's problems, as they begin to own the therapeutic process, converting it into a more collaborative effort.
- The reader should feel a connection to the character and feel safe to disclose their feelings and thoughts in the letter.

- The reader may then prepare a response to themselves from the perspective of the character.
- Essentially, the reader is writing to parts of themselves that they identify with in the protagonist.
- This perspective-taking enhances self-awareness, self-compassion and healing.
- For memoirs or other non-fiction, you may want to correspond with and write letters to the author or narrator.

Exercise

Pick a book that you've read recently and write a series of imaginative letters between yourself and the characters within the novel or the author. The letter-writing should follow a stream-of-consciousness approach, so just write whatever comes to mind, uncensored.

- First, choose a character or author to write to. Prepare a letter to them. You might want to start by acknowledging a connection you have with the protagonist or author or otherwise by acknowledging something that the protagonist or author has gone through that you empathise with. Is there a feeling or theme you are connecting with? Sadness, anger, fear, frustration, disappointment, betrayal, a loss, injustice? Whatever it is, write down what comes to mind and spend some time on your letter.
- After a short break, switch points of view and write back to yourself from the author or chosen protagonist's perspective.
- Reflect on these letters and consider what you might have

gained from this process, whether it's self-awareness, a coping strategy or a sense of resolution. How do you feel after writing the letters? What hopes do you have for the future?

Narrative Therapy – Key Takeaways

- Developed by Michael White and David Epston, narrative therapy emphasises the importance of personal narratives in shaping our identities and experiences.
- Key principles include externalising problems, deconstructing dominant narratives, constructing new ones and acknowledging multiple ones.
- It seeks to empower individuals to take control of their own stories and to construct more positive, hopeful and fulfilling life narratives.
- It's only in hindsight that we can make sense of what our story is through reflection, journaling and rewriting our narrative.
- Rewriting our story is important as it helps us find closure and even hope as we move forward again.
- It can encourage us to identify alternative stories and challenge outdated views and beliefs that no longer serve us.
- It can help us build self-esteem and re-establish a sense of self.

Exercise

1. **Putting together your narrative:** Start by writing your
    life story. This empowers you to find your voice, honour
    your experience, and pull together an understanding
    of the things in your life that have had a key impact on
    you and the meanings you have assigned to or derived
    from them.

2. **Externalisation:** Now detach the problematic
    behaviours or issues that you are facing from yourself.
    There should be a clear separation of the problem from
    who you inherently are (in other words, *you* are not the
    problem). For example, if you tend to feel angry, you are
    not necessarily an angry person. Instead, focus on how
    you can address these angry feelings. What is the cause?
    What can you do about them?

3. **Deconstruction:** Break down the story into isolated
    parts so that the problems identified begin to feel
    smaller, solvable and less overwhelming.

4. **Construction of alternative stories or outcomes:**
    Consider alternative stories, versions or outcomes that
    are different from your present story. For example, what
    could you incorporate into your daily life to address
    your anger? How would your life look if you were less
    angry? Your present story can prevent you from finding
    a different interpretation, leaving you feeling stuck.

Finding a different 'ending' or version of reality can positively impact decision-making, behaviours and our overall self-esteem.

8

SHANICE

> *'I am a Black woman. Don't look beyond me. Don't see
> through me. Look me in the eye. Hold my gaze. Listen to
> my heart. See my soul. See me for who I am, not what
> you would like me to be. Accept or reject but don't hide
> from my truth.'*

JANET AUTHERINE, *THE HEART AND SOUL OF
BLACK WOMEN*

*Client notes: Shanice H. is seeking representation. She wants
to read Black protagonists in fiction.*

'I want to read more *me*; I recently discovered how invisible I was,'
said Shanice.

It was shortly after the murder of George Floyd, and I was
receiving lots of requests from people who were looking to educate

themselves by reading more Black authors. Shanice's request was particularly striking. She wanted to read Black *British* authors, as she was British herself. She wanted to be seen, heard, valued, respected. She was seeking to fulfil these needs through books, because representation in books inks us on to the page. We are given space. We exist.

Shanice, who was in her early twenties, worked as an accountant at a prestigious accountancy firm. She'd been bullied at school and had always felt different as one of the few girls of colour in a private school. That difference left her self-conscious of her identity. She'd put on a mask to compensate for what she perceived as shortfalls in herself in the hope of seeking acceptance.

My question to her was, was *she* accepting of herself? Shanice was desperate to belong. I suggested *Queenie* by Candice Carty-Williams, a novel about a twenty-five-year-old culture journalist in a long-term relationship with her white boyfriend. Queenie's abandonment by her mother at age eleven haunts her throughout the narrative. Shanice could see herself in Queenie, in that she had abandoned herself, her identity, making herself invisible. She was just as complicit in her invisibility as the people around her. And beneath all that was a deep-rooted sense of shame, an entirely rational emotional response to circumstances that threaten one's self-esteem, social status and belonging.

'Shanice, I'm interested in learning more about your perspective on your racial identity. And I want to stress that this is a safe space to talk about any of your thoughts or experiences – and that includes whether you've ever felt uncomfortable or even ashamed?' I delicately probed.

As she thought about my question, she burst into tears.

'That's exactly what I have been feeling, all along. I have found it very hard to gain any social capital or standing in circles that are insufficiently diverse – essentially the ones that I have been exposed to all my life. I'm so used to being the token Black girl and it's painful.

'I feel angry, terrified, disheartened ... so many emotions. Flashes of hope along the way with an incredible amount of hard work have kept me going. For so long, I used to dream of waking up with silky hair and shimmering light blue eyes that would catch the attention of all the boys I wished I could date. It was all very silly and incredibly toxic.'

'There can be a sense of homelessness when we feel that we don't belong and that can be quite traumatic – depressing and demoralising,' I said.

Shanice's wish reminded me of Pecola in Toni Morrison's *The Bluest Eye* all over again, and my own experience of feeling invisible.

'Have you considered writing down how you feel, putting your thoughts on to paper? Perhaps into a poem?'

At my request, Shanice distilled her feelings into a confessional poem, a technique I use when clients have overwhelming emotions about something difficult. Expressing emotions helps remove the associated pain rather than storing it in the body, where it can inevitably settle over time, resulting in trauma.

WRITING CONFESSIONAL POETRY

WRITING POETRY – HOW IT WORKS

Writing confessional poetry provides us with the opportunity to express difficult emotions or something that might have felt forbidden.

Confessional poetry is a poetic style that emerged in the mid-twentieth century and is characterised by its deep introspection. This form of poetry focuses on the experiences, emotions, and inner struggles of the writer, often revealing intimate details about their life and psyche. It is often seen as a form of emotional catharsis for the writer, as it allows them to confront and express their innermost thoughts and feelings.

To write your own poem, refer to the guidance on Writing Poetry on pages 79–80.

In this case, Shanice, without realising it, held a deep sense of shame. Shame is a silencing emotion, as it makes us feel that what we have endured is our own fault. Shanice redrafted her poem several times, and this was the final version:

Ashamed.

Rejection. Shame. Despair.
The toxic triad rattling me.
Something's wrong with me.
A stinging stigma.

The way I look.
The way I speak.
The way I move.
Present but absent.

I cannot be seen.
An invisible cloak.
Completely enveloping me.
Prejudice stitching it together.

I'm ashamed.
Unconsciously I shrink.
My body hiding inside itself.
A lonely place to be.

Abruptly anger rises.
Striking rage.
The injustice of it all.
The unfairness of life.

Where is my humanity?
My dignity?

My respect?
As if I'm not a person.

Bitter, the tension builds inside.
I continue to rage.
Then the tears flow.
As sadness takes over.

Where do we go from here.
How do we get seen?
Unannexed?
I need a sign, I need hope.

I will rise. Strong like the sun.
I will be seen. Shining brightly.
I will be accepted. Embraced.
And I will do it with pride. Joyfully.

Shanice's confessional poem about the shame she felt around her racial identity acknowledged what she had endured and the painful emotions she held. Expression through poetry provided much-needed relief. Shanice felt lighter after writing it. After 'confessing', the burden of shame felt smaller. Feelings she'd held back for years – of hiding, of wanting to conform, of being ashamed about being different at school – were finally released, allowing her to embrace and accept her whole self.

I suggested she reread her poem several times. Each time she read it, she reported that the shame and linked feelings of despair, heartache and anger felt minimised. She felt open to embracing who she was. At the end of her poem, we can see her hope for a better future for herself.

Another book I thought Shanice would enjoy was Bernadine Evaristo's Booker prize-winning *Girl, Woman, Other*. It is a tribute to Black British womanhood and is told through the voices of twelve characters, each different and remarkable in her own way, weaving together a tapestry of their lives where there was once invisibility. I wanted Shanice to see herself in *all* twelve of the characters, and to realise that identity is fluid and there isn't only one way to be Black and British.

Through this book, I wanted to give her hope and a sense of belonging that she had missed in her childhood and teenage years. *Girl, Woman, Other* makes a clear statement: all women, regardless of race, are worthy and deserve to be seen. I wanted Shanice to internalise this, displacing the shame and despair.

To add to this, I also suggested she should try reading Malorie Blackman's series *Noughts and Crosses*. Malorie Blackman is one of the finest living Black British writers. Over the course of a remarkable career, she has authored over sixty books and was also the UK's Children's Laureate from 2013 to 2015. Through her writing, she has carved out space for Black British voices to be seen and heard. I wanted Shanice to connect with Blackman through her books – specifically, the *Noughts and Crosses* series, comprising six novels and three novellas. The novels are set in a segregated society in the twenty-second century, with Crosses (darker-skinned people) the ruling class, and Noughts (whiter-skinned people) the working class, mimicking the reality of the twenty-first century, just inverted. The Crosses are economically and socially powerful, while the Noughts are forced to exist within a system that will never be in their favour. Imagining a version of society that is so far from the reality we know throws into sharp relief the inequalities that exist within our own world. It offers us a fresh perspective on the possibilities of life and the agency we have to create a life that feels more equal. I didn't expect Shanice to read the whole series, but I was hoping that she would at least read the first book.

That day, Shanice went home feeling a little lighter after writing her poem. There was still more to be done. She was excited to read both *Girl, Woman, Other* and the *Noughts and Crosses* series. I could see the hope in her eyes. The world could be open to her and those who looked like her. What she now chose to do with her reading made all the difference.

When she returned for our second session, Shanice seemed in great spirits, and I was excited to hear more.

'Firstly, can I just say how much I loved the books you suggested.' She smiled, speaking fast, as though she had lots to tell me with very little time. 'I felt really empowered after reading about Amma's* Black theatre company. Although she wasn't welcome in the world of mainstream theatre, she still took every opportunity that came her way and made it her goal to create influential performances. I realised I can do something similar in my own life; it's inspired me to launch a collective for Black women in the City, where we can collaborate and make sure our voices are heard. Even after all these years, I feel like my hard work and ability hasn't been acknowledged, and as if I've simply been given a seat at the table because my company needed to tick a diversity box so that they could give themselves a pat on the back. I'm realising there's still so much to

---

*   Amma is the central character in the book, *Girl, Woman, Other*. She runs a theatre producing plays for Black women.

be done, and I can't continue to watch from the sidelines. I need to be the change I seek.'

'That's amazing.' I didn't want to say too much, as I was aware that in that moment, Shanice needed me to listen.

'But I think beyond this, I was fascinated to read about Black characters who felt othered by their race, but also how their class, gender identity and sexual orientation played into the way that they're perceived by others and how they see themselves. Evaristo's depictions of Black women felt both familiar and unfamiliar, but all the characters spoke to me and I felt safe in their company. These are women who, despite their own struggles, choose to be present for the people in their lives. Their connections to one another illustrate how connected we all are, and how much we can lift each other up. That was the inspiration behind my Black Women in the City Collective. It's got to the point where I've even been thinking about sending Evaristo an invite!' Shanice smiled.

'I am so happy to hear the positive impact the book had on you, Shanice.' I felt very maternal towards Shanice, and it made me so happy to know that she felt optimistic and hopeful after reading *Girl, Woman, Other*. Given such an enthusiastic response, I was curious to hear what she had made of *Noughts and Crosses*. 'And so what did you make of Malorie Blackman's writing?' I asked.

'It was really refreshing to read something incredibly imaginative and unconventional. Sephy and Callum's relationship actually reminded me a little of Shakespeare's *Romeo and Juliet*. These are idealistic young people who have grown up in a divided world that doesn't make sense to them. It was a stark reminder of how otherness helps no one, how division annexes even those with prejudice from their own humanity, and in the end only invites more fear and suffering. They were really helpful reads overall. I still need to read Carty-Williams's *Queenie* so I am looking forward to seeing what that might bring up.'

For Shanice, reading about people who represented her in literature meant reading about herself. It brought her experiences of being ignored and muted on to the page. She felt she'd been lifted out of the shadows and placed into a 'bright, sunny space, filled with warmth'. It was restoring. It brought connection. It brought validation. It brought awareness. All the elements of a therapeutic process.

In his book *The Self-Delusion*, psychiatrist and neuroscientist Gregory Berns wrote about how our self-identities are transient, always changing as we process new information both externally (from the world around us) and internally (from our memories and innermost thoughts and visions).[41] We can shape our inner protagonist. Berns conducted an experiment to see whether a book could truly alter our brains permanently, or at least effect long-lasting changes.[42] He arranged for a group of participants to read Robert Harris's *Pompeii*, which is based on the true story of the eruption of Mount Vesuvius in ancient Italy. This story was chosen due to its strong narrative. The protagonist observes steam around the volcano. Concerned, he returns to save the woman he loves, while the rest of the town's residents barely notice the signs of a pending eruption until tragedy hits. As part of the experiment, Berns divided the novel into nine sections and asked participants to read one section a day over nine days, finishing these in the evening and coming in the next morning to undergo resting-state fMRI (functional magnetic resonance imaging) scans. What he found was quite telling: often, the reader felt that they were in the body of the protagonist – or, to be more precise, the brain lit up under resting-state fMRI scans as though they themselves were experiencing the event they had been reading about. In this way, we take on the identity of the protagonist, leading to the theory that our brains are constantly adjusting and adapting, opening ourselves up to new possibilities and ways of being.

For Shanice, we had exposed the painful parts of her experiences that had been buried over the years. We were now taking time to attend to and treat her wounds, while giving them time to heal. It's a process.

I also wanted to help Shanice build a toolkit for future injuries to prevent them from inflicting pain or to help her manage them if they did happen. All the creative bibliotherapy practices in this book can form part of a future pain-management toolkit and offer wonderful ways to connect with ourselves and others. As we find connection, we also get in touch with our emotions and release them.

I wanted to leave Shanice with a few more hopeful texts to use in her future toolkit, written by authors from across the world and showing how people navigating racism have not only survived but also thrived. This included prolific American author Maya Angelou's *I Know Why the Caged Bird Sings*, Trevor Noah's *Born a Crime*, Nelson Mandela's *Long Walk to Freedom* and Margaret Busby's *New Daughters of Africa*.

To complement and balance these, I added further fiction by Black British authors including *Ordinary People* by Diane Evans, and Yvette Edwards's *The Mother*. Plus, she was looking forward to reading Candice Carty-Williams's *Queenie* later that evening.

Bibliotherapy Toolkit

Bibliotherapy techniques used: Writing poetry

Recommended for: Finding your voice, making sense of your feelings.

Books prescribed: Queenie by Candice Carty-Williams, Marjorie Blackman's *Noughts and Crosses*, Bernadine Evaristo's *Girl, Woman, Other*, Maya Angelou's *I Know Why the Caged Bird Sings*, Trevor Noah's *Born a Crime*, Nelson Mandela's *Long Walk to Freedom*, Margaret Busby's *New Daughters of Africa*, Diane Evans's *Ordinary People* and Yvette Edwards's *The Mother*.

BIBLIOTHERAPY TECHNIQUES APPLIED – KEY TAKEAWAYS & EXERCISE

Writing Poetry

See 'Writing Poetry – Key Takeaways' on pages 88–9.

Exercise

- Write a poem about an event that had a profound or surprising emotional impact on you.

- Talk about the feelings that came up for you, and why you chose to write about this event.
- Let your words flow; don't hold back or overthink the process. Write what comes to mind and focus on the writing and the poem itself. Remove all other distractions.
- Leave the poem for a while and come back to it later. Do you still feel the same? Edit it as necessary until you feel like your whole truth is sitting there on paper.
- Reflect on it and see how the poem makes you feel over time. Do you feel differently? Have you noticed any positive changes since writing the poem? Have you changed your behaviour in any way?

When we write poetry, and contain our emotions, desires and fears within it, the poem is also shifting something inside us. It's akin to a therapeutic intervention; it is addressing our painful memories and transporting us to a place of lightness and relief as our truth is expressed. This is the first step towards healing and inner peace.

9

REENA, DEVI, DEBORAH AND AMEE

'Give sorrow words; the grief that does not speak knits up the o-er wrought heart and bids it break.'

WILLIAM SHAKESPEARE, *MACBETH*

> ***Client notes:** A group of Asian mothers who've lost very young children or struggled with miscarriages.*

In addition to one-to-one bibliotherapy sessions, on occasion I will also work with small groups. I remember facilitating a group for Asian mothers who had lost young children or endured miscarriages as part of a local community initiative. Anyone who has experienced a bereavement will be able to tell you how life-shattering it is. Grief can come in many forms; it can shock, overwhelm, devastate, paralyse. It can incite rage and anger that then give way to an all-consuming sorrow. Above all, grief is messy, and there is no one way to deal with it. An individual process, it's ours alone to work through, yet the connection we feel with others who might be experiencing the same emotion is profound. Grieving in a group feels less painful than grieving alone.

In Indian culture, when a person passes away, their immediate family will gather with extended relatives and friends for the first ten to fourteen days, so that they are never left to mourn on their own; however, when it comes to a miscarriage, it's barely talked about, let alone mourned. Indian women who miscarry are shrouded in a cloud of shame that prevents them from processing their grief.

This bibliotherapy group comprised four women: Reena, Devi, Deborah and Amee. It was a small group designed to foster an immediate sense of intimacy to allow the mothers to feel safe. Reena was happily married, but had endured a miscarriage at the end of her first trimester. This baby would have been her first child. Although her husband had been a huge source of support, she struggled to discuss the loss with her extended family. Devi was from Wales and had been introduced to her husband through an arranged marriage. She had lost her three-year-old son in a tragic accident. Since his passing, she had given birth to another healthy baby boy. Deborah was Christian and deeply religious. She had a little girl of four, but was grieving a miscarriage that had happened six months earlier and still felt like a fresh wound. Although she had found solace in religious scriptures and her church community, she was still yearning. On some days, she found it all unbearable. She felt she had to live as two selves, which was exhausting – her exterior 'everything-is-fine self' and her 'mourning self'. Amee was the last of the group. Originally from Guyana, she had settled in the UK after meeting her husband and had suffered a miscarriage a year ago. She and her husband didn't really talk about it, and she was not motivated to try for another child. All four women were in their late thirties or early forties, and they had sought out little professional support. They felt that their experiences were not the kind of thing that was really talked about within their community, despite how common these punishing losses were. Their losses were not normalised in any way, and that compounded the feelings of shame and heartache even more. When I explained how bibliotherapy worked and that we would be focusing on poetry therapy, which is an excellent tool for groups, the women were intrigued.

POETRY THERAPY IN GROUP BIBLIOTHERAPY

GROUP BIBLIOTHERAPY – HOW IT WORKS

Group bibliotherapy is a form of therapy that involves using literature or written materials to help individuals explore their emotions, thoughts and behaviours in a supportive group setting.

In a group bibliotherapy session, a facilitator or (biblio) therapist selects texts, such as novels, poems or personal essays, that are relevant to the group's needs and interests. Participants are then given time to read and reflect on the selected material individually or as a group. The facilitator may provide prompts or questions to guide the group's discussion or encourage participants to share their thoughts and feelings about the material.

Through the discussion of the literature, participants may gain new insights into their own experiences, learn from the experiences of others, and develop new coping strategies or ways of thinking about their challenges.

Group bibliotherapy can also provide a sense of community and social support for individuals who may feel isolated or alone in their struggles.

Benefits of Group Bibliotherapy

- **Self-expression in a group:** Expressing ourselves in a group allows our voices and feelings to be heard, witnessed and acknowledged. This can be therapeutic and healing, and helps individuals build their self-esteem and confidence.
- **Creativity:** Writing down or discussing our reflections engages our creative faculties, which promotes healing. Creativity requires a state of mindfulness that induces relaxation and helps individuals become more aware of their thoughts and emotions, leading to greater levels of self-awareness and problem-solving.
- **Connection:** Sharing our reflections and/or writing can help individuals feel more connected to others in the group. This can help build empathy, understanding

and support among group members as well as creating a sense of belonging. This also encourages group motivation and commitment to the therapy process.

- **Reflection:** Individuals give and receive feedback, enhancing their self-awareness, giving them insights and improving their understanding of old coping strategies while learning new ones.
- **Diversity of thought:** Different perspectives offer a more comprehensive understanding of a theme or issue that is being discussed, enabling more informed decisions and opinions from a carefully considered position.

LITERARY REFLECTIVE PRACTICE USING POETRY – HOW IT WORKS

'We would allow the champion of poetry – men who do not practise the art themselves, but are lovers of it to offer a prose defence on its behalf, showing that poetry is a source not only of pleasure, but also of benefit to communities and to the life of man.'

PLATO, *REPUBLIC*

To engage in literary reflective practice using poetry, apply the Literary Reflective Practice Framework on page 74.

Why is Poetry Therapy Effective in Group Bibliotherapy?

- Poems are the right length to read and discuss in one group session.
- The immediate access poetry gives us to our emotions allows group members to connect and share their feelings, enabling discussion and reflection within one group session.
- These feelings can then be discussed and further reflected upon in the next session after members have had some time to consider them between sessions.
- Group members are also encouraged to write their own poetry in response to the poem they have read, allowing expression of thoughts and emotions through writing. This relieves pain and can lead to catharsis, both for the person writing the poem and also for other group members who can resonate with the poem and benefit from the discussion of shared experience.

After polite introductions, we began by creating a trust contract. We made it clear that everything that was discussed in the group would stay within the group. With the ground rules set, I introduced the women to our first poem, John O'Donohue's 'For Grief'. We took it in turns to recite the verses. The poem was striking. The ladies discussed how profoundly O'Donohue had captured their feelings of grief, as though he had lived their nightmare too. They shared that there were days when life felt liveable again, and then out of the blue, grief would rear its ugly head, and they were back in its grip. 'No one really knows what has been taken from you.' This truth, highlighted in the ninth line of the poem, was perhaps the most profound. It was fascinating to watch these women, who had so struggled to speak about their turmoil with friends and extended family, opening up to one another and speaking freely of their pain. The external pressures that had silenced their grief seemed to melt away in this space, as each member of the group suddenly found themselves with others who *did* know what had been taken away, women who had walked their path and in their shoes. There was a deep sense of connection, and the group began to relax as they realised that they were in a safe space in which they didn't have to deny their grief. There was no room for shame, judgement and guilt.

As we spoke, Amee noted that unlike the others she found it hard to express any sadness. She felt this was the reason why she and her husband had been ignoring their grief, as well as the conversation of trying for another baby.

I probed a little more. 'Have you always found it hard to express your sadness?' I asked gently.

'Yes.' She nodded. 'I barely cry. It's too much for me.'

'When was the last time you cried?' I asked, curious.

'Properly cried? I remember how upset I was when my mother died. I was only four years old, and after her passing, my grandmother looked after us instead. There were four of us; I was the second youngest. I had only been two years old, my younger sister six months, when my father left, and then my mother died two years later.'

'That must have been a really devastating experience for a four-year-old to go through,' I said softly.

'It was. It was heartbreaking,' Amee agreed calmly.

Devi began to cry, tears streaming down her cheeks. 'I'm so sorry. I just think about my own son and I could never imagine him having to live without me.'

Amee, although calm, was a little taken aback that Devi felt so strongly about her mother passing away. This often happens in groups. We begin to carry the painful emotions of others, shouldering them and expressing them for the members who are overwhelmed. Devi was doing that for Amee. Amee had trouble expressing sadness as it most likely took her back to her childhood and the loss of a mother whom she had not yet fully grieved. She had a lot of crying and grieving to do – for the deep loss she felt as a result of her mother's absence, and also for the miscarriage. I wanted Amee to reflect on this before the next group session – on expressing the pain and sadness she was holding on to from these significant losses.

For the next session, I asked the women to write a personal response to John O' Donohue's poem 'For Grief', as well as another of his poems that we discussed, 'On the Death of the Beloved', so that we could share and discuss these at the next session.

'Write down whatever comes to mind,' I guided them. 'It could be a thought. A word. Phrases. Quotes. Feelings. Memories, stories. Book titles. Helpful advice. You could even write a poem. Whatever it is, just write – write as though no one will be reading it. It's your safe space. And remember, you only share what you feel comfortable with. We are not here to judge or criticise. One more thing: if the writing does not come to you, then feel free to record your feelings in a voice note. Sometimes it's easier to say what we're feeling rather than to write it down.'

As we ended the session that day, we noted that their initial nervousness had eased, and that they already felt more relieved.

We gathered again a week later, on a sunny Wednesday in October. It was unseasonably warm. The group of four arrived on time. There's a certain magic with group therapy; everyone is always on time. I think it's the feeling of connection and community; you want to be able to show up for the people who have shared their pain so openly with you.

The synchronised energy in the room felt like a godsend. While no one came in bright and cheery, raring to go, there was a tranquillity and peacefulness that suggested the women felt comfortable in the space and with one another. Their own words, captured in their journals, reminded them that their feelings were not forgotten but would be witnessed and validated by the group in their upcoming session. This is the power of group bibliotherapy.

Deborah always had lots to say. She was perceptive and often listened to her intuition.

She began, 'I read both O'Donohue poems and also reflected on our past session. And boy, there was so much to share. The overriding feeling I had was that I was less alone. Suddenly, I had a space of my very own where I could be angry and *feel* my pain. It was a relief. I realised that, like Amee, I had never *done* anger before. I had never been taught how to express anger. In my family, we were always about doing the right thing and staying calm and feeling grateful. While these were all great virtues, anger was an emotion that was always minimised, something to fear rather than feel. As I reflected on O'Donohue's "On the Death of the Beloved", there was so much I wanted to share, but here's something that I have chosen from my journal.'

She read out:

John O'Donohue's poem 'On the Death of the Beloved' is a heartfelt meditation on grief, loss and the enduring power of love. The poem speaks to the deep sense of loss and sorrow that accompanies the death of a loved one and offers words of comfort and hope to those who are mourning. The words rang terrifyingly true for me, and [helped me with] acknowledging the enormity of my loss, and the sense of emptiness and darkness that I felt. O'Donohue speaks of the deep connection that we have with those we love, and the profound sense of absence that is left behind when they are gone. As the poem progresses, O'Donohue begins to explore the idea that even in death, love endures.

He speaks of the way that our loved ones live on within us, in the memories we hold and the love that we continue to feel for them. He encourages us to cherish these memories, and to find comfort and solace in the knowledge that our loved ones are still with us, in some sense, even after they have passed on.

In response to O'Donohue's poem, Deborah wrote a poem of her own:

It felt earth-shattering.
My feet could not feel the ground.
My eyes tight, stretched.
Reacting to the danger I felt.

Then it was true.
The child was no more.
It can't be, I screamed.
It was. It really was.

My stomach fell.
I wanted to scream forever.
Because nothing could appease my anger.
It was infinite.

After what felt like an eternity the tears came.
And just like O'Donohue's rope of grief,
The last one arrived, my eyes sore.
I acknowledged my loss.

You were there in my soul.
You were there in my breath.
You were there in my heart.
You were in my bones.

One day I know we will be together in a different form.
We will return to each other.
Perhaps invisible, perhaps in space.
Reunited. Forever.

Striking, honest, open. The other women nodded their heads in agreement. The power of the words shifted something in Deborah, and she began to cry.

'I want to let myself cry today. I need to. I am going to take every opportunity to express my sadness.'

As Deborah said these words, Devi began to cry too, and there were exchanges of tears, hugs and tissues. It was a cathartic moment. I wanted it to last for as long as it needed to. This is where the work happens. The pain is lifted. No longer in your body, in your mind or on the page. It dissipates into the air.

The group came together again in silence. Devi wanted to go next. Nervously, she cleared her thoughts and began reading from her journal.

O'Donohue's 'On the Death of the Beloved' really triggered something inside me. My little boy's love was like the dawn – it brightened my day. The sound of his voice was music for me and sometimes it still haunts me as though he is just there, ready to tell me not to worry, not to cry. 'Mummy, I'm still here. I always was. You have just had a terrible nightmare!' If only it were true, my sweetie.

O'Donohue seemed to pick out these little details that ring true for a grieving mother. He really knows what it's like to lose someone, and that made me gush – a waterfall of pain washed down. Who knew where it was going, my tears were flowing fast. Slowly, the tears stopped, and I felt a warmth coming from my little boy, wherever he was, inspiring me to find courage to live each day to the fullest. Comforting me and consoling me, reassuring me.

O'Donohue implies in his poem that one day he will be reunited with his son; I too am waiting for that day. I make peace every day with your absence, knowing that we will be together again soon. And that is the vision I hold in my mind. Of reunion. It's my way of coping and staying strong. That vision is the light at the end of this dark road for me.

As she finished, Devi seemed more confident and reassured.

While still calm, Amee's eyes glistened with tears. Although these remained firmly in the corner of her eyes, refusing to roll down her face, I sensed a real shift. She had started the grieving process. This was particularly important, as she found it so hard to express her sadness. And now she was *feeling*. This is half the work of therapy, to be able to give yourself the permission to *feel*.

'I am so glad to see you honouring your sadness,' I told Amee. I did not want to interrupt the process, nor did I want her to feel self-conscious or exposed, in case the discomfort overwhelmed the grief.

Encouraged, Amee decided she wanted to go next, and shared her reflections eloquently in her lovely, silky-smooth voice:

For me, the lightbulb moment from the last session was the realisation that I don't feel sadness. That I am too scared to. That it's too painful and that I often shy away from it. Therefore, I used the poems to focus on bringing forward feelings of sadness. Initially, this exercise felt quite difficult, and for a while I was numb and nothing was coming to mind. So instead I read the poems out loud and then voice-recorded how I felt immediately after.

'For Grief' resonated with me the most. The oscillation Donohue describes – days when you wake up happy, and then the moment breaks and you suddenly find yourself on this black tide of loss. I feel this inconsistency all the time. It's worst when I am on my own. These ups and downs are so painful. I'm falling apart and collecting myself a lot. Then I feel like I am not allowed to feel this. I need to be strong for my husband, for the rest of my family, just like how I was when my mum passed away. I looked after my little sister and practically raised her myself. So, I brush these painful feelings aside, distracting myself with food and music and exercise. I have now realised that I was dodging these uncomfortable feelings.

When I listened to the voice recording again, I burst into tears. Listening to my own pain gave me the permission to cry. It was powerful. I suddenly knew what I needed to do in that moment. The voice notes allowed me to empathise with myself. This way of connecting with myself seemed profound. I think, going forward, this is how I will be processing emotion when I am struggling.

Reena, the shyest of the group, joined in and quietly read from her journal:

For me, the biggest takeaway has been that there was nothing to be ashamed about. It happens to so many of us. Why should we be stigmatised or blamed for what's happened? Hearing the experiences of everyone here, I felt I wasn't alone, nor was it a failure on my part. I'd felt so inadequate for so long. This happens to many women, but when we don't talk about it, we feel as though this horrible, unfair thing has happened and we must carry the weight of the pain alone, the shame crushing us. As though there's something wrong with us. But none of us did anything wrong. It wasn't our fault that we lost our children. Why should we have to feel embarrassed when something awful has happened? Why aren't we consoled instead? Why isn't there more support? Why do we have to feel shame when what we need to do is grieve?

For the first time, I could focus on the actual loss. Like in O'Donohue's poem 'On the Death of the Beloved', I felt myself connecting with Amira [*the name she had planned to give the baby*], as though she had made it to this world. Although I never got a chance to meet her, I had experienced the energy she brought. She brightened up my life, bringing colour to those dark days. Now I can feel her in the rhythm of my breath. She is close by. We will reunite at some point in the future, and this gives me comfort and joy and a different kind of hope.

Through their journaling and reflecting on the poetry, the group had begun to uncover an underlying theme in all their writing and reflections: finding a way to keep alive their connections to their loved ones who had passed. It was no surprise that this was the case. In his book *Grief Counselling and Grief Therapy*, grief researcher William Worden discussed the four tasks that one must complete in order to process grief, with the final one being, 'to find an enduring connection with the deceased in the midst of embarking on a new life' (the first three are: 'to accept the reality of loss', 'to process the pain of this loss' and 'to adjust to a world without the deceased').

This theme of keeping alive their connection to their lost loved ones was a recurrent longing that seemed permanently etched in the minds of these four astonishingly brave and beautiful women. In light of this, I felt it apt to finish with Rumi's 'The Window':

Your body is away from me
but there is a window open
from my heart to yours.
From this window, like the moon
I keep sending news secretly.

I managed some smiles and some bittersweet tears, but I felt that these women had progressed in their grief in some way. They now had the gift of poetry to turn to whenever they wanted an emotional outlet or something to help them recall how important their feelings were instead of suppressing them or feeling there was no room for their expression. They could now heal through poetry and reflection, and by sharing their thoughts with people they trusted.

Reena felt less ashamed of her miscarriage, and able to talk about it openly. Deborah began to express her anger more, realising the importance of this and actually learning *how* to, having suppressed it for so many years. Devi began to hold positive visions in her mind, inspired by poetry that brought hope, helping her make peace with her grief but also other life challenges. Amee had started her long overdue journey of navigating sadness, something she had rejected for more than three decades. Poetry and group connection had been the catalysts for their healing journeys.

Bibliotherapy Toolkit

Bibliotherapy techniques used: Group bibliotherapy, poetry therapy, literary journaling.

Recommended for: Processing feelings of grief, shame, anger, sadness, disappointment and loneliness. Also helpful for finding a sense of closure.

Poems Prescribed: John O'Donohue's 'For Grief' and 'On the Death of the Beloved', Rumi's 'The Window'.

BIBLIOTHERAPY TECHNIQUES APPLIED – KEY TAKEAWAYS & EXERCISES

Group Bibliotherapy – Key Takeaways

- Group bibliotherapy uses literature or written material to help people explore their emotions, thoughts and behaviours in a supportive group setting.
- A facilitator or therapist selects literature relevant to the group's needs and interests, and participants reflect on the material both individually and as a group.
- The group discusses the literature, sharing their thoughts and feelings and gaining new insights into their experiences.

- Group bibliotherapy can provide social support and a sense of community and belonging for those who feel isolated.
- Connecting with others in the group by sharing our reflections and writing can lead to empathy and understanding, enhancing group motivation and commitment.
- Diversity of thoughts allows for a more comprehensive understanding of a theme or issue, leading to more informed decision-making.

Exercise

This is a group exercise for readers who might be part of a book club or who wish to participate in a meaningful, intimate group discussion with family or friends using literature.

- Choose a piece of writing that is relevant to your group's need and interests. This could be a novel, a short story, a poem or a personal essay. For example, if the group is dealing with grief and loss, you could choose a poem like 'Immortality' by Clare Harner.
- Ensure that everyone in the group has a copy and allow ample time for everyone to read it. Encourage people to underline or highlight any passages that resonate with them or that they find particularly meaningful.
- Once everyone has had a chance to read the material, ask them to share the thoughts and feelings that it evoked. You could use prompts like:
  - *What emotions does this piece of literature evoke for you?*
  - *Are there lines or passages that really stand out to you? Why?*

- ○ *How does this literature relate to your own experiences?*
- ○ *What insights or lessons can you take away from this literature?*
- Encourage everyone to engage with each other's comments and to share their own perspectives. You could facilitate a group discussion, or you could break the group up into smaller pairings for more intimate conversations.
- As the organiser, be present to listen to the group's comments and provide support as needed. Offer validation and encouragement to guide the discussion towards positive and empowering themes.

By engaging in this exercise, participants can explore their emotions, connect with others, and gain new insights and perspective.

Literary Journaling – Key Takeaways

See 'Literary Journaling – Key Takeaways' on pages 82–3.

Writing Poetry – Key Takeaways

See 'Writing Poetry – Key Takeaways' on pages 88–9.

Literary Reflective Practice Using Poetry – Key Takeaways

See 'Literary Reflective Practice – Key Takeaways' on pages 82–3.

CHAPTER 10

LEO

'We are the visionaries, inventors, and artists. We think differently, see the world differently, and solve problems differently. It is from this difference that the dyslexic brain derives its brilliance.'

TIFFANY SUNDAY, *DYSLEXIA'S COMPETITIVE EDGE*

Client notes: Leo M. is eight years old and struggles to read due to dyslexia.

'The letters are jumping at me!' moaned Leo. 'I don't want to read anymore! I'm tired!'

Leo was an eight-year-old boy at a state primary school in leafy north London. His mother, Suzanne, had first picked up on his dyslexia when he started bringing reading home. His teachers noticed he struggled with his 'b's and 'd's and jumbled his letters when spelling:

'there' would be 'three', 'heart' would be 'hreat', 'wheel' would be 'whele'. He knew all the answers to his sums, except he'd write the numbers the wrong way around. He'd been assigned a special educational needs coordinator who helped him at school and ensured he had the right support in place. Suzanne later confirmed the diagnosis through a private assessment.

'His friends at school all giggle and poke fun at him when he's asked to read aloud, and he can't bear it,' Suzanne explained. 'They'll often get carried away into a sing-song: "Leo's a silly reader, Leo's a silly reader!"'

Since so much of school life revolves around reading, I could hear the frustration and despair of both Leo and his mother. Suzanne had been following a podcast I had recorded with a speech and language therapist titled, 'Raising a Reader & Storyteller',* that was about developing a young person's love for reading. She was fascinated by bibliotherapy and thought it might be something that could help Leo address some of his reading difficulties and reduced motivation, as well as the emotions he was dealing with: the frustration, the disappointment, the shame and the drop in confidence as he muddled through literacy lessons at school.

Leo was a bright boy with an astounding vocabulary. The only thing he couldn't do was bring together this incredible knowledge on the page. The words danced at him and he could not pin them down, resulting in mispronunciation or him finding it too painful to even look at the page as 'the words played tricks'.

That morning, Suzanne had brought him to see me in the hope that we could build up Leo's confidence, get him interested in books, and

---

*   The 'Raising a Reader & Storyteller' podcast can be found here: https://www.audible.co.uk/pd/Raising-A-Reader-Storyteller-Podcast/B08JK1T4Q7

alleviate the pain and shame he felt when it came to reading and writing. While he was receiving additional one-to-one support at school, she wanted him to engage with reading in a different way, one that would allow him to heal and find joy, comfort and understanding.

LITERARY REFLECTIVE PRACTICE USING GRAPHIC NOVELS

Immediately, I thought of graphic novels. They are the perfect confidence-building tool for reluctant readers, as they capture kids' attention through captivating illustrations and storytelling while avoiding the tedious working-through that children reading more text-based books are required to do. Graphic novels can also easily broaden a child's vocabulary, as the illustrations make it easier to understand and grasp the language used. We can use the story and context to work with the emotions they prompt in children, working through issues that might otherwise have been hard for a child to verbalise.

LITERARY REFLECTIVE PRACTICE USING GRAPHIC NARRATIVES – HOW DOES IT WORK?

Graphic narratives, comprising graphic novels and graphic memoirs, make the perfect therapeutic literature for both adults and children. While comic books have been around for the last hundred years,[43] a new subgenre of graphic stories has arisen known as graphic pathographies,[44] which are essentially physical- or mental-health narratives presented in a graphic format. These graphic pathographies offer readers insights into their own illnesses as they relate to the protagonist's personal experience of the physical illness or mental health condition. They've been effective in the mental health field, helping people who struggle with depression and post-traumatic stress disorders.[45] For example, the graphic novel *Maus* by Art Spiegel depicts the horrors of the Holocaust through anthropomorphic characters and explores intergenerational trauma and survivor's guilt, while Guillaume Singelin's *PTSD* explores the reality of being a war veteran struggling with trauma after returning home from a difficult war.

In this way, graphic narratives also promote mental health literacy,[46] providing insight into mental health issues and themes and offering an opportunity for readers to learn more about their own mental health illness or issue, while also validating their own understanding and experience of it.

Graphic narratives also excel at capturing groups of 'reluctant readers'. Many young people and adults who have little interest in reading still enjoy graphic novels or graphic memoirs. These groups may have lower literacy skills and smaller vocabularies, but they can improve these skills through reading these graphic narratives.

How Do Graphic Narratives Aid the Therapeutic Process?

- Through visual storytelling, graphic novel narratives go beyond the linear prose of traditional novels in capturing the true social experience of the narrator or artist, capturing gesture, movement and happenings in time, making them more engaging and immersive than traditional novels.[47]
- The use of images and words allow readers to more readily connect and empathise with the story, author and/or artist on an emotional level.
- Graphic novels invite the discussion of mental health issues more easily through images and words that would otherwise be too difficult or painful to discuss directly.

Using Literary Reflective Practice with Graphic Narratives

To engage in literary reflective practice using graphic novels, apply the Literary Reflective Practice Framework on page 74.

Use of Graphic Novels for Children

Graphic novels aimed at children often feature a hero protagonist who initially faces an obstacle or crisis of some sort that they are able to overcome through perseverance. These stories observe the power of perseverance, and see the hero progress to find new possibilities or solutions for problems that initially seemed overwhelming or too difficult to address.

Young readers resonate with the crisis the hero faces and the associated feelings. Since the exploration of these feelings is indirect, the child feels safer, less exposed. There's no judgement. The child understands what these emotions are, either in name or experience, and this promotes the development of emotional literacy. As the child reads on, the story affects them both consciously and unconsciously (which is where the real therapeutic work happens) and they find new, lasting ways of coping, of dealing with the problem and of being.

Often, the child realises that their previous coping strategy (bottling things up, showing aggression towards others, giving up/not caring, or even succumbing to and accepting abusive behaviours) are no longer working, and they're invited to welcome and embrace healthier coping strategies. In this way, the graphic novel, in the frame of a therapeutic story, has changed the child's perception of themselves and their situation.

The child's awareness and understanding grow, leading to eventual adoption of these strategies, and these become lifelong skills for coping with life's challenges.

Literary Reflective Practice with Children

Children may require prompts and discussion when using literary reflective practice with graphic novels. Use the exercise and prompts at the end of this chapter to guide you.

I was going to take a two-pronged approach with Leo. I planned to gently ease him into reading by starting with a book that would tackle some of the shame he felt at school and help him gain some confidence in reading again. We were going to call on the graphic novel versions of Rick Riordan's *Percy Jackson and the Olympian* series. The protagonist of the book, Percy Jackson, has always felt a little different to the rest of his friends, and it's revealed that this is because he is the son of a mortal mother and the Greek god Poseidon. I hoped that seeing Percy experience exclusion would prompt Leo to discuss his own feelings of isolation, especially when Percy realised that the isolating difference was his superpower.

The pictures helped Leo connect words and sentences much faster and gave him the visual space to master the story without slowing down the pace. We worked through the book together, and I was there to offer support whenever he needed it. I asked some guided questions to bring into focus Leo's emotions. We wanted him to have the emotional vocabulary not only to discuss the books he was reading, but also to process them. Story is really the first language of children. They often find it difficult to talk directly about their feelings and experiences, as often they don't have the vocabulary and command of language required. Stories offer a gateway, as the use of images, metaphors and characters are an important tool in which to communicate their feelings and emotions to us.

'How do you feel about Percy?' I asked Leo.

'I feel sad for him. If he was real, he could easily be my friend,' said Leo animatedly. 'I understand how he feels. I feel that too.'

'When do you feel sad, Leo?' I asked gently, wanting to hold that space.

'Sometimes when I struggle to read in front of others,' said Leo, looking down and not making eye contact.

'That's okay. You're allowed to feel sad and to take your time with reading,' I reassured him. 'We are all growing and developing at different paces.'

Leo nodded but said little else. Sadness can feel intensely painful for children, and they often choose to ignore it. I could see that was what Leo was doing. He started flicking through the pages of *Percy Jackson and the Lightning Thief*, fidgeting a little. Then he dug deep into his pocket and pulled out a small Rubik's cube.

I wanted him to focus and bring him back to his feelings by using the language of images and expression.

'I can understand how difficult, unfair and challenging that can feel,' I said. 'Often in those times we can feel alone and a little unsure of how to deal with the situation in the moment. It's almost like no one has ever told you how to be or what to do, when people behave in ways that are hurtful to us.'

Something had piqued Leo's attention, and he was listening more intently now. I drew him back to the story, as I did not want to lose this moment. When we discuss things clinically with children, they can often lose interest. Instead, I wanted to use Percy's story in *The Lightning Thief* to prompt helpful, therapeutic conversation. The mind has an uncanny ability to engage in emotional issues through storytelling. The use of imagination and the unconscious mind allows us to bring together images and feelings to express what we are experiencing rather than simply engaging in a two-way conversation that might not be as powerful at processing emotions; in this way, we can marry all our feelings from the past to the present and reconcile and repair.

'Tell me one thing from the story that has really stayed with you,' I said.

'When Annabeth told Percy that he was running away, I realised that maybe I was running away from the problem and the kids who were upsetting me.'

'That is a natural reaction,' I reassured him. 'The situation might have felt scary or a little threatening, and to protect yourself, you feel like you had to stop reading in front of them and perhaps go into your shell.'

'Yes, that's exactly how I felt,' he responded enthusiastically, as though somebody had read his mind. 'Scared, sad, and…'

'And possibly ashamed?' I suggested.

'Yes, I was embarrassed and disappointed.' He looked at his shoes, again feeling as though he had done something wrong.

'Shame is a very difficult feeling. But there is a way to deal with it.' I smiled, hopeful. 'Shame is like a beautiful wildflower that's too scared to bloom in the garden for fear that it's unwanted and will be treated as a weed. But you can't control where a wildflower grows, in the same way that you cannot control how you grow and develop. Just because its blossoming is unexpected, it does not make the flower any less beautiful. We are all unique. Do you think Percy felt shame?' I asked.

'I think he did.' Leo nodded. 'I feel inspired by him because he has dyslexia like me. He realised that he is supposed to read ancient Greek, and that's why the words looked mixed up. Maybe that's what's happening to me.'

Leo had found new perspective and hope on the page. It was not all doom and gloom. He was willing to look at his dyslexia in a new light. He was able to self-soothe and refuse to let the issue diminish his sense of self-esteem and who he was. He was able to separate himself from the feelings of shame, not letting them define him. This was the first step towards overcoming and processing shame.

The use of the flower metaphor to explain shame was very helpful for Leo. It really engaged his imagination and gave him imagery and symbolic language to get to the heart of how he was feeling. He was reminded that, like the flower, he was no less of a person – and certainly not a 'bad' person – just because he was different. Metaphors, like stories, can suspend judgement because they engage the imagination and tap in to our emotions, allowing us to experience a situation from a novel perspective, while still containing universal themes and messages that resonate with us on a deep emotional level.

Both are wonderfully powerful therapeutic tools that, when used correctly, get us to the crux of the emotion in a profound and meaningful way. Often, children have what British psychoanalyst and writer Christopher Bollas referred to as 'unthought knowns'. This is where we have not assigned a meaning or label to an experience, but we intuitively *know* what it is. It is what we feel when we hear a piece of music that touches us or when we watch a deeply moving film. Stories create this same sort of incredibly profound experience for children. When we begin to give language and words to that experience, we start to feel understood and can become aware of why the story is resonating with us.

NARRATIVE THERAPY

'If you could be the hero of your own story, just like Percy was, what story would you write?' I asked Leo.

'All my friends and I would be on holiday in a hot country, maybe Spain, and we would be swimming in the pool. And then Rafi [*Rafi is one of the boys at school who makes unhelpful comments about Leo's reading*], who can't swim properly, falls into the pool. No one else notices except me, because I always spot things! Mum tells me I am very good at spotting things, things that other people don't see except me. I manage to jump in and save Rafi. Rafi is so grateful to me after that, he becomes kinder. And I become the person who would spot things that other people don't see. That is my superpower.

'The other children, in return, would help me with my reading and I would help them find things they have lost or help them in other ways. I am very good with my hands, too, and fixing things. I love to help my friends fix their toys when they are broken.

'My reading would be amazing, too! Everyone would listen carefully to me as I read. I would be a superstar!'

Here, Leo has created his own story to solve a problem he is facing, and has reached a happy ending where he feels confident in himself. He is a 'superstar'. He feels more optimistic and hopeful about life.

This is an example of narrative therapy: a story we write about ourselves to gain closure, to assimilate what has happened to us, to process and embrace it, and to come to terms with the outcome. Leo's story was glowing with hope at the end. He seemed to embody courage and optimism throughout his narrative. And the positive ending highlighted his confidence and resilience. This is the benefit of narrative therapy, and why it's a great technique to use with young children, who are more open to optimistic endings. The best things we can teach them are how to find closure when closure is not readily available, and how to live life from a position of optimism, while still acknowledging and validating the negative emotions we might have once felt.

Exploring open, guided questions prompted by a graphic novel gave us a meaningful conversation that led Leo to discover a series of insights about himself, helping him to realise he could get through things no matter how difficult they might seem at the time. Like Percy, Leo felt he could be bold and brave and become the hero of his own story.

Coincidentally, Rick Riordan's own son struggled with dyslexia and ADHD, and so he decided to turn his son into the hero of his own story. Riordan's understanding and nuance has allowed the series to resonate with many neurodiverse readers as well as neuro-typical ones.

At the end of our work together, Leo's mother reported that he seemed more calm, resilient and able to cope with peer pressure at school. He seemed confident, and motivated to read and write again. Graphic novels became a coping strategy. He even created his own characters, with the goal of writing his own graphic novel about a young boy who used reading to conquer his fears. Leo's reading continues to improve, and his mother continues to use guided questions relating to graphic novels and narrative therapy as supportive tools for Leo's mental well-being.

Bibliotherapy Toolkit

Bibliotherapy techniques used: Reflective practice using graphic narratives, narrative therapy.

Recommended for: Anxiety, depression, neurodiversity and understanding illness.

Graphic novels prescribed: Percy Jackson and the Olympians: The Graphic Novels series.

BIBLIOTHERAPY TECHNIQUES APPLIED – KEY TAKEAWAYS & EXERCISE

Reflective Practice Using Graphic Narratives – Key Takeaways

- Graphic narratives comprise graphic novels and graphic memoirs. A subgenre of graphic stories, graphic pathographies (physical or mental health narratives presented in a graphic format) offer readers insights into their own experience of physical illness or mental health conditions.
- They promote mental health literacy and an opportunity for readers to learn more about their own mental health illness or issue.

- Graphic narratives appeal to 'reluctant readers' and readers with lower literacy skills.
- They are perfect for capturing the true social experience of the narrator or artist, making them more engaging and immersive than traditional novels.
- The use of images and words allow readers to access their emotions more readily.
- They make it easier to discuss difficult or painful subjects.
- See 'Literary Reflective Practice Framework' on page 74. If working with children, try using guided questions and prompts to help them with their literary reflective practice – see the exercise below.

Exercise

Let your child or teenager select a graphic novel that they feel connected to. Use the following questions to kickstart a discussion about feelings and thoughts:

- What made you choose this book?
- Would you like to meet any of the characters in this story? Why?
- Do any of the characters remind you of someone you know?
- If you could be any character in this story, who would it be?
- Which character would you like to be friends with? Why?
- How would you help the character in the story?
- What made you happy in the story?

- What made you feel sad?
- What might happen to the main character(s) at the end of the story?
- Are there any questions you'd like to ask any of the characters?
- How do you think the main characters are feeling as the story develops?
- What makes the character happy? What makes them sad or scared?
- How did the characters change as the story progresses?
- Is there an anti-hero or villain in the story? Is there anything you liked about them?
- What was your favourite part of the story and why?
- Is there a part of the story that made you feel uncomfortable, worried, scared or angry?
- Does the story remind you of your own story or situation in any way? If yes, how?
- How would you have liked the story to end?
- How would you change the story, if that was something you could do?
- Have you learned anything new or different after reading the story?
- Did the story surprise you in anyway?
- What do you think the moral of the story is? Or the lesson that the author wants you to take away from the story?
- Did you enjoy the story? Would you recommend it to your friends?
- Is there a story in which you'd like to be the hero? And if so, what is it?

If helpful, get your child or teenager to draw how they are feeling. If working with young children, get their toys out and assign characters to them. By recreating an emotional experience through story, drawing or play, children can express their truths from a safe distance, and far more easily than through their limited, everyday emotional vocabulary, which might be quite primitive at this stage.

Stay with the child's feelings; don't persuade them to feel otherwise or dismiss their feelings. It's really important to sit with your child, no matter how painful, as this is the only way they learn to regulate their emotions.

At the end, summarise their discoveries by reflecting back how they felt. Remember to ask them what they learned and whether they might implement a plan of action based on this (including new behaviours and coping strategies). Examples of this are teaching your child or teenager:

- How to be open to love while still learning how to set boundaries that are protective.
- How to embrace change and be open to operating in a different way.
- When to pick your battles. Sometimes, it's best to let go and accept the situation, but at other times, it's important to challenge and confront the situation.
- You have the right to say 'no', to be yourself and/or to be different.
- You have the power to change how you feel.
- You have the right to be free of fear or worry.

Narrative Therapy – Key Takeaways

See 'Narrative Therapy – Key Takeaways' on page 166.

Exercise

Suggest creating a story with your child where they are the hero of the story. Give them the following prompts:

- What is the problem or the issue?
- How are they feeling?
- Is there anyone else in the story? What happens to them?
- How do they solve the problem?
- How would they like the story to end? And how do they feel at the end?

Discuss the story at the end, and let your child be as creative as they would like, even if the story does not make sense. Stay with the story, and reference characters in the story when discussing an event in the narrative. For example, 'How lonely for the little boy that he was having to deal with all of this on his own.'

Emotional vocabulary for children

Beyond the basic feelings of angry, sad, happy, scared and so on, the following expressions might also be useful when talking to young children or referencing what characters in a story are feeling:

- feeling alone/lonely
- feeling annoyed
- not feeling wanted
- feeling left out/not included
- missing someone
- feeling cross
- hating someone or something
- feeling things are not fair
- feeling that something hurts too much
- feeling confused
- feeling disappointed
- feeling like it's all too much
- feeling like 'I don't want to be here'
- feeling as if nobody cares
- feeling like 'I can't seem to do anything right'

Storytelling allows children to cross over into the threshold of their imaginations, where they can explore their feelings freely. Simply reading or hearing words might not always speak to their emotions in the same way. Using our imaginations gives us access to our unconscious too, where we are free to be, explore and think creatively and intuitively as well as to express ourselves more readily. Storytelling is the perfect medium through which a child can start exploring and building their own personal narrative: one that allows them to feel empowered, optimistic and free of the feelings that might previously have been holding them back.

PART III

The Art of
Literary Curation

*'I can never read all the books I want; I can never be
all the people I want and live all the lives I want. I can
never train myself in all the skills I want. And why do I
want? I want to live and feel all the shades, tones and
variations of mental and physical experience possible in
my life. And I am horribly limited.'*

SYLVIA PLATH, *THE UNABRIDGED JOURNALS OF
SYLVIA PLATH*

11

SELECTING A BOOK

THE READER IN MIND

In his book *The Unknown Unknown – Bookshops and the Delight of Not Getting What You Wanted*, Mark Forsyth argues that 'the best things are the things you never knew you wanted until you got them'.[48] It is this feeling of satisfaction and delight that I aim to create in my clients and readers.

Not knowing what you might get creates a sense of anticipation, and this instils excitement in the reader. Online algorithms can't mimic the unpredictability of the bibliotherapy process, as recommendations are based on what you like to read and books that you've enjoyed in the past; in short, they are not programmed to think outside the box. This is why the work of a bibliotherapist is so important: curation is at the heart of what we do. My job goes beyond the internet, bookstores and libraries, and involves talking to people, to other mental health professionals, to teachers, to social workers, to *readers* everywhere. Most importantly, it requires a depth of understanding of and compassion for the reader in front of me.

Selecting literature is an art form, a fine-tuned skill requiring judgement, adaptation and an accommodation of the reader. For some readers, it's purely the combination of therapeutic techniques being brought to life through reading that facilitates relief and psychological healing. For others, it's the pleasure of the exercise, the escapism, the creativity, the space, time and distance that reading gives them.

Through gentle questions and prompting, the bibliotherapist can learn about the reader's motivations and begin to know them more intimately. This enables them to recommend literature that meets the reader's needs, preferences and goals. Although bibliotherapists generally try to avoid recommending books that the reader may have already read, in some situations it can be useful for the reader to revisit vital passages of certain texts, or information that they may find helpful in the situation they are currently in.

THE ART OF LITERARY CURATION

What Kind of Text Are You Looking For?

The word curator comes from the Latin word '*curare*', which means 'to take care of' and was initially used in the context of looking after ancient Roman bath houses. Nowadays, it's often used to refer to the curation of objects and art for collections at galleries and museums. Just as an art or museum curator carefully and thoughtfully pulls together meaningful objects for an exhibition, I treat every book prescription or reading list request with the utmost thought and care, aiming to create something unique and valuable for my readers. What are the themes emerging that will be helpful for my readers? What books will go well together? What authors and writing styles will the reader enjoy? Will they have enough time to read these based on their current circumstances? Is a long novel, a shorter novella or even a short story collection more appropriate? Is the medium of the books suggested fit for purpose (e.g., paperback, hardback, eBook, audiobook)? Are the books diverse enough? Do they provide sufficient representation? Is the reading list balanced, or do they prefer to only read one type of genre?

It's about literally putting yourself in the reader's shoes, inhabiting their world and seeking as much context as possible. What issues are they facing? How are they feeling? What would they like me to focus on? Are they seeking something therapeutic? Do they want to heal? Do they want to be transformed by the literature? Or do they crave escapism? A literary sanctuary?

Connection to the text, the author and the writing style is always at the forefront of my mind. Will the reader actually resonate with the author's writing? Will it engage them? Will they feel that they have found a familiar friend in the author? This is often informed by the authors, genres and books they have previously loved – from a client's reading history, I can form a strong sense of what they might enjoy.

In the introduction to his book *Everything and Less: The Novel in the Age of Amazon,* author and literary critic Mark McGurl says that to read generically is to read repetitiously – a desire that we develop as young readers and continue into adulthood.[49] Initially, it's a desire to read our favourite stories over and over again; later, it's a desire to read similar stories. Therein lies an important clue about what we are compulsively seeking. After all, as McGurl astutely observes, every act of reading is primal, and returns us to the bedtime stories that we fell in love with as children with our primary caregivers by our sides. There might be a desire to be loved (the romance genre), or to be seen (memoir), or to escape into realities more exciting than ours (fantasy).

Should all of this inform their future reading? All these questions can make a subtle difference between selecting something like Glennon Doyle's *Untamed* or Florence Williams's *Heartbreak* for someone who is seeking a memoir after a bitter divorce. Both books are incredibly true to the experience of divorce, but they tackle it in strikingly different ways. Whose writing style is the reader going to connect with more? Williams's writing is uplifting, hopeful and addictive, laced with stories, research and anecdotes. Doyle, on the other hand, is insightful and writes incredibly accurately about the experience of divorce. She examines the questions we are afraid to ask, truly empathising with our inner needs, fears and desires. All these considerations go into the selection process.

How Much Time Do You Have to Read?

Time is one of the biggest constraints to reading. If you're reading one book, you're saying no to another, because of the limited time we have. If we are lucky, we may average 4,880 books in our lives.* In a world where there are more than 100 million books, it's easy to grow anxious over the lack of time we have for reading. Life is literally too short to read everything we would like to, and so our to-be-read pile grows and grows, acting as a physical reminder of all the books we'll never read. And yet, we'll walk into a bookshop and spot another book that's calling out, *'Read me instead! You'll enjoy me more!'*, and thus the cycle continues. So how do we break the pattern and ensure that we're choosing books that are worth our time, that will enrich our lives, that will offer a sense of wonder – and, well, that we'll actually read?

CURATING A READING LIST

Drawing on my experience as a bibliotherapist, having helped a range of readers with diverse reading tastes, I've created a series of questions to help you to start creating a to-be-read pile that will actually be read. You can also use this to curate a reading list for a friend or family member:

---

*   This is based on a survey by Emily Temple, managing editor at Lithub, who used data from the Social Security Life Expectancy Calculator and the Pew Research Centre to calculate the average number of books read by men and women over their lifetimes (assuming men live to eighty-two years old and women to eighty-six years old), and also what reader 'classification' they fell into, such as 'average reader', 'voracious reader' and 'super reader'. The 4,880 books refer to the greatest number of books read on average, by female 'super readers' who live to be eighty-six years old. For male 'super readers', the greatest number of books read on average was 4,560. For voracious readers, these numbers were 3,050 and 2,850 books respectively, while for the average reader, they were 732 and 684 books respectively. Temple, E. (2017). 'How Many Books Will You Read Before You Die?'. lithub.com.

- What issue(s) are you currently facing? What is your current situation? Is there a specific issue that you'd like to focus on?
- How are you currently feeling?
- What would you like to get out of the personalised book prescription/bibliotherapy session?
- What is your reading preference? (For example, fiction, non-fiction, poetry, philosophy, etc.)
- How much time can you devote to reading?
- What are your favourite books/authors?
- What are your preferred reading mediums? Do you prefer to read on an eReader or listen to audiobooks? Or do you prefer hardback or paperback books?
- Is there anything else we should know?

The Book-Selection Process

To determine what books the reader will connect with, I use a further seven checkpoints. I consider whether the texts chosen mirror the feelings, interests and goals of the client and if the selected literature fits the clients' preferences.

- Would the story resonate with the client in terms of allowing them to connect with the text and explore their feelings, needs, interests and goals?
- Do the characters show coping skills and resolution?
- Are there any other additional actions/exercises that the client should complete alongside the reading of the text? For example, literary journaling, writing a letter or poem,

or recording voice notes about how they felt during the reading of the text?

- How has this book been received by a general audience (based on professional and public reviews, ratings and opinion pieces, and client feedback)?

Many times, I have come across books that I know I won't connect with, so I have learned to filter out the red herrings and to say no to books that I won't enjoy. We already have so many demands on our time – from work to family commitments to friends – that we should only be saying yes to books that we know will enrich our lives. I call this my 'Reading Intuition', a feeling in my gut when I instinctively know that something I am reading won't work for me.

How Do You Develop Your Reading Intuition?

- Simply having more reading experiences can help you develop a sense of the style, writing, genre and reading medium you personally prefer. A 2010 study found that experience in a particular domain can help individuals develop more accurate and reliable intuition in that domain.[50] The study looked at the intuitive decision-making abilities of firefighters and found that those with more experience were better able to make accurate and efficient decisions under pressure.
- Mindfulness meditation can boost decision-making abilities, according to a study following individuals who

practised mindfulness meditation over an eight-week period. Those who meditated had increased intuition and improved decision-making ability compared to a control group.[51]

- Reading more widely across a diverse range of literature can help readers develop a more accurate and reliable intuition of the literature that they will enjoy.

Sometimes when we reflect, we realise that there are books that we just don't connect with, and that's okay too. Sometimes the themes of a book may be triggering for the reader. And sometimes we fall short of reading time. In all these instances, I'll suggest alternatives. For example, if a reader is time-poor, the most valuable or meaningful thing I can suggest is a short story or essay, something they can get through in one sitting. Occasionally, I'll ask my clients to be open to books that they might not otherwise read, as introducing a wild card can offer readers a new perspective that will enable further self-reflection.

I often collect reviews and feedback from readers and clients, of books they have either loved, or could not get past the first chapter. This data over time has helped me develop my own intuition and understanding of what might work for one reader but might be completely inappropriate for another.

The Serendipity of Book Discovery

Sometimes a client will come to a session with a book already in hand. It might be a book that a friend had mentioned to them and suddenly seemed to be everywhere they looked, or a book they spotted someone reading on the train that called out to them. For whatever reason, they felt it was a book they really needed at the time. This is the serendipity of book discovery. There's definitely a place for these books in the bibliotherapy process, and they are wholeheartedly embraced.

Of course, the work isn't done once we've created our reading lists; in fact, it's only just begun.

HOW TO BUILD A READING HABIT

Once you've identified the books that you know you'll enjoy, using my prompts, make a promise to yourself to actually carve out time to read. Think of this as an important act of self-care.

One of the most common questions I am asked is: 'How do I incorporate reading into my busy lifestyle?'

My response is always, 'How do you incorporate exercise? Or any regular habit that's important to you?'

It's the making of that *regular* commitment every day. It has to be daily – the *toothbrush test*. If you read daily, you are more likely to keep reading daily for life. Otherwise, you'll end up a holiday reader. There's no in-between.

Here are a few tips for building a reading habit.

- Reading for fifteen minutes a day, whether it's on your commute or at bedtime, can help you build a routine reading habit. Research on habits suggest it takes anywhere from eighteen to 284 days for a habit to become entrenched in our lives.[52]
- Be *intentional* about it. Switch off social media, Netflix, video games – whatever the distraction – and focus on reading.
- Audiobooks are great when you're on the go.
- Find a reading partner and hold each other accountable.
- Set yourself a reading challenge.
- Consider the *instant* benefits to your mental well-being and stress levels that reading can bring – see below.

The Impact of Reading on Stress Reduction

In 2009, a research study conducted by neuropsychologist Dr David Lewis at the University of Sussex found that reading for six minutes a day reduced stress levels by sixty-eight per cent. In contrast, listening to music reduced stress levels by sixty-one per cent, having a cup of tea by fifty-four per cent, taking a walk by forty-two per cent and playing video games by twenty-one per cent, so reading appeared to be the superior form of stress reduction compared to any other leisure activity.[53]

I believe that to read is to become literate in ourselves, in humanity and in the wider world. Reading heals and provides pleasure simultaneously. It grounds us in reality, but immerses us in fantasy too. It allows us to explore the heights of our imaginations, but also the depths of our sorrows and misfortune. It acts as a mirror, showing us ourselves and our blind spots, but when we need it to nurture or save us from ourselves, it also takes us down rabbit holes that become our saving graces when life's challenges become too much. It provides social connection through rich and diverse characters when we need it the most, but also offers us a quiet space when we are seeking more solitary pastures.

With all that literature and reading affords us, my question to you, the reader, is: *How will you leverage the benefits of reading in your lifetime? Are you ready to embrace all that reading can bring, from self-discovery to personal transformation and well-being, by prioritising books that bring value, enjoyment and meaning?*

12

AN A–Z OF BOOK PRESCRIPTIONS

'To read is to dream, guided by someone else's hand.'

FERNANDO PESSOA, *THE BOOK OF DISQUIET*

There is something compelling about reading lists. I wonder if it's because, in a world overwhelmed by literature, where we are short of time, they gives us a clear road map for reading up on a particular theme, knowing which books would be the most relevant, valuable or enjoyable. Or is it the anticipation of what one might be able to read on a particular subject or theme? Book titles, covers and blurbs hook our imaginations and let us enjoy the fantasy of the book before we even start reading. Then there's the promise of a book and what it might deliver for us, whether fulfilling a therapeutic need or satisfying a personal interest.

This is the power of the reading list. Yet we also know that the reading list will always be incomplete, that there could always be one more book we could add or suggest or recommend. As a bibliotherapist, I have to make peace with this shortfall, in the hope that I have prioritised the most relevant and beneficial texts for my readers.

With this in mind, I wanted to share my own reading lists of recommended books, arranged in A–Z format categorised by mental health and well-being themes. I fondly call these 'book prescriptions'. My lists were partly inspired by the wonderful work of bibliotherapists Ella Berthoud and Susan Elderkin, founders of the bibliotherapy service at The School of Life and authors of *The Novel Cure: An A–Z of Literary Remedies*,[54] who have played an important role in helping to popularise the practice. I hope you find my suggestions helpful and valuable as well as uplifting, engaging and inspirational. More of these can be found at booktherapy.io/pages/a-z-of-book-prescriptions. You can also put in a request for a theme not found here by emailing us at hello@booktherapy.io.

A

Abandonment

We're all likely to experience feelings of abandonment at some point in our lives – perhaps in the form of a bad break-up, the loss of a trusted friend, or lack of support from a parent – and this can hugely affect our mental well-being and leave us feeling lonely and distressed. If we don't give voice to our emotions, they can end up festering and affect our self-esteem and our ability to trust in future relationships. You might find the following books helpful in exploring your feelings of abandonment.

Fiction
David Copperfield by Charles Dickens (novel)
The Days of Abandonment by Elena Ferrante (novel)

Non-fiction
What My Bones Know by Stephanie Foo (memoir)
Home is Where We Start From by D.W. Winnicott (psychology, essays)

Abusive Relationships

Sometimes in life, we find ourselves or a loved one in an abusive relationship. This is a type of relationship where one partner uses various forms of power and control to maintain dominance over the other partner. This can be in the form of physical, emotional, verbal, financial and/or sexual abuse. The following books can help us identify and understand the dynamics of abuse, develop coping strategies, and establish healthy boundaries. They can also help us recognise our own strengths and build resilience, to move forwards in a positive and empowered way.

Fiction
Paper Butterflies by Lisa Heathfield (novel)
A Little Life by Hanya Yanagihara (novel)
A Woman Is No Man by Etaf Rum (novel)

Non-fiction
Consent by Vanessa Springora (memoir)
Heart Berries by Terese Marie Mailhot (memoir)
He Promised He'd Stop by Michael Groetsch (self-help)
Better Boundaries: Owning and Treasuring Your Life by Jan Black (self-help)

Where to Draw the Line by Anne Katherine (self-help)
The Courage to Heal: A Guide for Women Survivors of Child Sexual Abuse
    by Ellen Bass and Laura Davis (self-help)

Addiction

Addiction occurs when we develop a compulsive and repetitive pattern of substance use or behaviour despite negative consequences. Although it can involve substances, such as drugs or alcohol, or particular behaviours, such as gambling, sex or internet use, addiction can take many less common forms. Many of my clients have found the following titles useful in exploring addiction, but if you think you might be engaging in behaviour fuelled by addiction, please ensure that you speak with a healthcare professional.

Fiction
Postcards from the Edge by Carrie Fisher (novel)
NW by Zadie Smith (novel)

Non-fiction
Terry: My Daughter's Life-And-Death Struggle with Alcoholism by George
    S. McGovern (biography)
We All Fall Down: Living with Addiction by Nic Sheff (memoir)
The Biology of Desire by Marc Lewis (psychology, neuroscience)
Facing Shame: Families in Recovery by Merle A. Fossum and Marilyn J.
    Mason (psychology)
Beyond Addiction: How Science and Kindness Help People Change by Jeffrey
    Foote (psychology)
Unbroken Brain: A Revolutionary New Way of Understanding Addiction by
    Maia Szalavitz (psychology)

Never Enough: The Neuroscience and Experience of Addiction by Judith
    Grisel (psychology)
Dopamine Nation: Finding Balance in the Age of Indulgence by Dr Anna
    Lembke (psychology)

Ageing

Ageing is a privilege, but it can also feel frustrating, distressing and
lonely to experience a gradual decline in our bodies. However, with the
right resources, we can navigate the ageing process with greater wisdom
and understanding, improving our ability to cope with the changes
we're going through. These books on ageing bring uplifting insights
on later life and how we can live a life filled with social connection and
optimal health, while preserving our self-worth and dignity.

Fiction
A Man Called Ove by Fredrik Backman (novel)
These Foolish Things by Deborah Moggach (novel)

Non-fiction
Nothing to Be Frightened of by Julian Barnes (memoir)
Can't We Talk about Something More Pleasant? by Roz Chast (memoir)
The Art of Aging, A Doctor's Prescription for Well-Being by Sherwin B.
    Nuland (health)
Being Mortal: Illness, Medicine and What Matters in the End by Atul
    Gawande (health)
What Are Old People For?: How Elders Will Save the World by William H.
    Thomas (health, sociology)

Anger

Anger can be a useful expression of feelings of hostility, frustration and irritation, and it can also encourage us to dig deeper to understand why we're feeling the way we are and to pinpoint the root of our anger. The following selection of titles will allow you to explore your anger in a healthy and safe environment.

Fiction
Fight Club by Chuck Palahniuk (novel)
The Grapes of Wrath by John Steinbeck (novel)
The Road by Cormac McCarthy (novel)
The Bell Jar by Sylvia Plath (novel)
The Color Purple by Alice Walker (novel)

Non-fiction
Anger: Handling a Powerful Emotion in a Healthy Way by Gary Chapman (self-help)
Never Get Angry Again: The Foolproof Way to Stay Calm and in Control in Any Conversation or Situation by David J. Lieberman (self-help)
The Dance of Anger by Harriet Lerner (self-help)

Anxiety

Fear, worry or uneasiness are all natural responses to future events or uncertain outcomes. But when these emotions are excessive and persistent, and interfere with your daily life, it's important that you acknowledge them and speak to a professional. Symptoms of anxiety vary widely, but include restlessness, irritability, difficulty concentrating, muscle tension and sleep disturbance. I've curated a selection of titles – including fiction, workbooks and practical guides – that have worked best for my clients, but please be sure to discuss this with a health professional too.

Fiction
Turtles All the Way Down by John Green (novel, young adult)
I Was Born for This by Alice Oseman (novel, young adult)

Non-fiction
Dare: The New Way to End Anxiety and Stop Panic Attacks Fast by Barry
        McDonagh (self-help)
My Age of Anxiety: Fear, Hope, Dread, and the Search for Peace of Mind by
        Scott Stossel (self-help)
The Anxiety & Phobia Workbook by Edmund J. Bourne (self-
        help, workbook)
The Anxiety and Worry Workbook: The Cognitive Behavorial Solution by
        Aaron T. Beck and David A. Clarke (self-help, workbook)
From Panic to Power by Lucinda Bassett (self-help)
Notes on a Nervous Planet by Matt Haig (therapeutic non-fiction)
*Don't Feed the Monkey Mind: How to Stop the Cycle of Anxiety, Fear, and
        Worry* by Jennifer Shannon (self-help)
Don't Panic: Taking Control of Anxiety Attacks by Reid Wilson (self-help)
Wabi Sabi: Japanese Wisdom for a Perfectly Imperfect Life by Beth Kempton
        (self-help)

B

Body Image Issues

Each day, we are faced with hundreds of seemingly perfect airbrushed images in advertisements and on social media, and this can seriously affect our self-esteem and our relationship with our bodies. If you've noticed that you're engaging in persistent negative self-talk when it comes to your body, please consider speaking with a professional. I've also found that the following books are useful tools to better understand body image and our often-fraught relationship with our bodies.

Fiction
How Moon Fuentez Fell in Love with the Universe by Raquel Vasquez
    Gilliland (novel)

Non-fiction
The Body Is Not an Apology: The Power of Radical Self-Love by Sonya Renee
    Taylor (psychology, sociology)
Body Talk: How to Embrace Your Body and Start Living Your Best Life by
    Katie Sturino (self-help, workbook)

Boundary-Setting

Setting boundaries is often challenging for a variety of reasons. If we have a history of people-pleasing or conflict avoidance, we may worry that setting boundaries will upset others and lead to some form of confrontation. We may feel guilty for being selfish and asserting our own red lines at the expense of the expectations of the people around us. However, boundaries are an essential part of self-care and actually allow us to maintain healthy relationships. As daunting as it might seem, we can learn to develop our assertiveness and address any negative emotions around boundary-setting. I've found the following non-fiction books are excellent guides on boundaries.

Non-fiction
Boundaries by Dr Henry Cloud & Dr John Townsend (psychology)
Where to Draw the Line by Anne Katherine (psychology)
Daring Greatly by Brené Brown (self-help)
Set Boundaries, Find Peace by Nedra Glover Tawwab (self-help)

Bullying

Bullying can have a significant impact on our mental health and cause a range of emotions to surface, including loneliness, disconnection, anger, shame and fear. It can also leave you feeling anxious, depressed and worthless, so it's important to confide in someone you trust. Regardless of how you are made to feel in the moment, everyone deserves to be treated with kindness and respect. If you are in the process of healing, you may find the following books comforting.

Fiction
Wonder by R. J. Palacio (novel)
Thirteen Reasons Why by Jay Asher (novel)
Blubber by Judy Blume (novel)

Non-fiction

Please Stop Laughing at Me: One Woman's Inspirational Story by Jodee
    Blanco (memoir)

*It Gets Better: Coming Out, Overcoming Bullying, and Creating a Life
    Worth Living* edited by Dan Savage and Terry Miller (essays,
    testimonials)

Burnout

Burnout is an increasingly common condition, particularly for those
who work in a high-pressure environment and/or in professions
that require long hours, intense focus and a high level of emotional
engagement. A lack of support, conflicting demands and poor
work–life balance can all lead to burnout. It's important to recognise
the signs of burnout and take steps to prevent or address it, such
as taking breaks, practising self-care, setting boundaries, seeking
support, and making changes to your work habits or lifestyle. The
following books provide excellent strategies for coping with the
symptoms of burnout and designing a life that promotes a healthier
work–life balance.

Fiction

There's No Such Thing as an Easy Job by Kikuko Tsumura (novel)

Non-fiction

Emotional Female by Yumiko Kadota (memoir)

Burnout: The Secret to Unlocking the Stress Cycle by Emily F and Amelia
    Nagoski (self-help)

Designing Your Life: How to Build a Well-Lived, Joyful Life by Bill Burnett
    and Dave Evans (self-help)

Four Thousand Weeks: Time Management for Mortals by Oliver Burkeman
     (personal development)
Atomic Habits by James Clear (personal development)
Deep Work: Rules for Focused Success in a Distracted World by Cal
     Newport (personal development)

C

Cancer Care

A cancer diagnosis can feel incredibly overwhelming, partly because
we still do not know what causes the majority of cancers. Treatment
can often feel like trial and error, so it's only natural to feel anxious,
uncertain, lonely, resentful and frustrated. Your doctor will be able
to offer in-depth advice and coping methods to navigate this complex and difficult illness, but you may also find other people's stories,
whether fictional or true, reassuring and comforting.

Fiction
Maps of Our Spectacular Bodies by Maddie Mortimer (novel)
The Fault in Our Stars by John Green (novel)
Ways to Live Forever by Sally Nicholls (novel)
My Sister's Keeper by Jodi Picoult (novel)

Non-fiction
When Breath Becomes Air by Paul Kalanithi (memoir)
The Emperor of All Maladies by Siddhartha Mukherjee (health)
The Immortal Life of Henrietta Lacks by Rebecca Skloot (biography)

Career Concerns

Sometimes we may find ourselves questioning the path we've taken, asking ourselves: is this really what I want to do for the rest of my life? What is my true purpose? It might be that we're worried about a skills gap that we have, or perhaps there are simply limited opportunities in the field we've chosen. Another concern I often hear from clients is how difficult it is to navigate a toxic work environment – especially when feeling disempowered by a lack of support from their manager. Economic downturns or technological changes can also threaten job security. The following books offer a space for reflection and exploration of our career goals, including discovering our purpose and the type of work we might find meaningful.

Fiction
Black Buck by Mateo Askaripour (novel)
Happy for You by Claire Stanford (novel)
Microserfs by Douglas Coupland (novel)
Pastoralia by George Saunders (novel)

Non-fiction
I Could Do Anything if I Only Knew What It Was: How to Discover What You Really Want and How to Get It by Barbara Sher and Barbara Smith (self-help)
David and Goliath: Underdogs, Misfits and the Art of Battling Giants by Malcolm Gladwell (psychology)
Drive: The Surprising Truth About What Motivates Us by Daniel Pink (psychology)
What Color Is Your Parachute? by Richard N. Bolles (psychology, personal development)

Work Won't Love You Back by Sarah Jaffe (self-help)
Lost in Work: Escaping Capitalism by Amelia Horgan (philosophy, sociology)
How to Find Fulfilling Work by Roman Krznaric (self-help)
The Second Mountain: The Quest for a Moral Life by David Brooks (philosophy)
How to Change the World: Social Entrepreneurs and the Power of New Ideas by David Bornstein (social change, entrepreneurship)
Uncanny Valley by Anna Wiener (memoir)

Caring

Looking after others can be a rewarding and fulfilling experience, but also a challenging and demanding one, requiring time, effort and patience. Common emotions experienced are stress, exhaustion, frustration, guilt and sadness. Balancing our own needs versus the needs of those we care for can be extremely challenging. It's important to take time out for ourselves and seek the support we need to prevent burnout. Being a carer can also feel quite lonely; to alleviate some of this isolation, here are some novels and non-fiction books about other carers whose stories and experiences might resonate with our own.

Fiction
Purple America by Rick Moody (novel)
Eileen by Ottessa Moshfegh (novel)
The Caregiver by Samuel Park (novel)
The Story of a New Name by Elena Ferrante (novel)

Non-fiction

Creating Moments of Joy: Along the Alzheimer's Journey by Jolene Brackey
(health, psychology)

*They're Your Parents, Too!: How Siblings Can Survive Their Parents' Aging
Without Driving Each Other Crazy* by Francine Russo (self-help)

The Reluctant Carer: Dispatches from the Edge of Life by
Anonymous (memoir)

Tender: The Imperfect Art of Caring by Penny Wincer (memoir)

Coming Out

For many people, coming out can be a difficult and emotional process, involving revealing a part of themselves that they may have kept hidden for years and the fear of potential rejection from friends, family or wider society. At the same time, coming out can also be a liberating experience. It allows us to live our lives authentically and openly and to connect with others who share similar experiences and identities. It's important to remember that everyone's coming-out experience is unique. If you're wondering how best to approach it, the following novels and memoir might offer insight, hope and courage.

Fiction

The Velvet Rage by Alan Downs (novel)

Giovanni's Room by James Baldwin (novel)

Fun Home by Alison Bechdel (graphic memoir)

Call Me by Your Name by André Aciman (novel)

Non-fiction

Trans by Juliet Jacques (memoir)

Courage

Courage requires a positive mindset: a combination of determination, bravery and confidence. Typically associated with taking risks or facing fear, it involves a willingness to overcome difficult challenges or obstacles. Seen as an emotional response to adversity, it can lead to personal growth and accomplishment. If you're struggling with finding the courage to pursue something that might be positively life-changing, these stories might help you find your own inner power and courage.

Fiction
The Help by Kathryn Stockett (novel)
Speak by Laurie Halse Anderson (novel)

Non-fiction
Wild by Cheryl Strayed (memoir)
Brave Enough by Cheryl Strayed (quote collection)

D

Depression

Depression, characterised by feelings of sadness, hopelessness and a loss of interest or pleasure in the things we once enjoyed, is a serious mental health condition, so it's important to seek appropriate professional support and guidance tailored to your own unique experience of depression. If, at the same time, you want to explore what it means to live with the condition through literature, you may find the following books helpful.

Fiction
Mrs Dalloway by Virginia Woolf (novel)
Veronica Decides to Die by Paulo Coelho (novel)
Looking for Alaska by John Green (young adult)
Psychiatric Tales by Darryl Cunningham (graphic novel, autofiction)

Non-fiction
Furiously Happy: A Funny Book About Horrible Things by Jenny Lawson (memoir)
The Noonday Demon: An Atlas of Depression by Andrew Solomon (psychology, memoir)
Girl, Interrupted by Susanna Kaysen (memoir)
Reasons to Stay Alive by Matt Haig (psychology, memoir)
The Upward Spiral by Alex Korb (psychology, neuroscience)
Unholy Ghost: Writers on Depression edited by Nell Casey (essays)
The Cognitive Behavioral Workbook for Depression by William J. Knaus (psychology, workbook)
Marbles: Mania, Depression, Michelangelo and Me by Ellen Forney (graphic memoir)

Poetry
Depression & Other Magic Tricks by Sabrina Benaim (poetry collection)
Lost in my Mind by Riley Kinkade (poetry collection)

Divorce

Going through a divorce is an incredibly difficult process that is fraught with numerous challenges, from grieving the relationship we once had – it's valid to mourn even if it was your choice to end your marriage – to uncertainty regarding the future. There are legal and financial implications and social stigma too, but taking time to read about other people's divorce journeys can allow us to feel less alone and reduce the stigma and uncertainty we feel.

Fiction
Fleishman Is in Trouble by Taffy Brodesser-Akner (novel)
Heartburn by Nora Ephron (novel)
Fates and Furies by Lauren Groff (novel)

Non-fiction
This is the Story of a Happy Marriage by Ann Patchett (non-fiction)
Heartbreak: A Personal and Scientific Journey by Florence Williams
    (science, psychology)
Aftermath: On Marriage & Separation by Rachel Cusk (memoir)
Eat, Pray, Love: One Woman's Search for Everything by Elizabeth
    Gilbert (memoir)

Poetry
Changing with the Tides by Shelby Leigh (poetry collection)

E

Envy

Although we often think of envy and jealousy as interchangeable, envy refers to the desire to possess something that another person has, while jealousy is a fear of losing something that you already possess. It's very common and natural to feel small pangs of envy from time to time, but it can also be an acutely painful and powerful emotion. If you're struggling to keep your envy in check, you may want to explore some of the following novels that feature envy as a key theme, as well as some non-fiction books that provide direct guidance on navigating envy.

Fiction
Looker by Laura Sims (novel)
Madame Bovary by Gustave Flaubert (novel)
The Sun Also Rises by Ernest Hemingway (novel)

Non-fiction
Envy: A Theory of Social Behaviour by Helmut Schoeck (psychology)
Status Anxiety by Alain de Botton (philosophy)

F

Family Dynamics

Every family is unique and has its own stories and challenges. From personality clashes to intergenerational trauma, mental health issues and financial stress, these difficulties impact our family dynamics. However, knowing you're not alone and that every family has some sort of issue can be comforting. The following literature explores family dynamics across fiction and non-fiction, and offers strategies for positively shifting the family dynamics in which we find ourselves.

Fiction
Far from the Tree by Robin Benway (novel)
My Name is Lucy Barton by Elizabeth Strout (novel)

Non-fiction
Educated by Tara Westover (memoir)
The Glass Castle by Jeannette Walls (memoir)
What We Carry by Maya Lang (memoir)
They F*** You Up: How to Survive Family Life by Oliver James (psychology)
Family Healing by Salvador Minuchin (family therapy)
Every Family Has a Story: How We Inherit Love and Loss by Julia Samuel (psychology)
Far from the Tree: Parents, Children and the Search for Identity by Andrew Solomon (psychology, parenting)

Fatherhood

Fatherhood marks the dawning of an incredibly exciting new chapter in life. It can bring significant change and new challenges, so if you're feeling nervous about how to navigate this new role, here are some wonderful novels and memoirs that explore what it means to be a father, what to expect and how to address some of the challenges you might come across.

Fiction
Room Temperature by Nicholson Baker (novel)
To Kill a Mockingbird by Harper Lee (novel)
Bewilderment by Richard Powers (novel)

Non-fiction
Between the World and Me by Ta-Nehisi Coates (memoir)
The Role of the Father in Child Development by Michael E. Lamb
    (psychology)
Home Game: An Accidental Guide to Fatherhood by Michael
    Lewis (memoir)
Things My Son Needs to Know About the World by Fredrik
    Backman (memoir)

Female Empowerment

Female empowerment has been explored in numerous works of literature. Here are some notable books on the subject. These offer diverse perspectives and can help readers gain a deeper understanding of the issues facing women today.

Fiction

The Power by Naomi Alderman (novel)
Circe by Madeline Miller (novel)
Body of Stars by Laura Maylene Walter (novel)

Non-fiction

Year of Yes: How to Dance It Out, Stand in the Sun and Be Your Own Person by Shonda Rhimes (memoir)
Becoming by Michelle Obama (memoir)
Men Explain Things to Me by Rebecca Solnit (feminism, essays)
If Women Rose Rooted: A Journey to Authenticity and Belonging by Sharon Blackie (feminism)
We Should All Be Feminists by Chimamanda Ngozi Adichie (feminism, essays)
Women Who Run with the Wolves by Clarissa Pinkola Estés (feminism, psychology, philosophy)

Poetry

Great Goddesses: Life Lessons from Myths and Monsters by Nikita Gill (poetry collection)

Finding Meaning

When it comes to finding meaning, we can turn to literature as a guide. The writing we consume often invites introspection, encouraging us to reflect on and consider our beliefs, values – and the way we see the world. The following books in particular are invaluable tools for discovering meaning and purpose in our own lives.

Non-fiction

Man's Search for Meaning by Viktor E. Frankl (memoir, psychology)
The Untethered Soul: The Journey Beyond Yourself by Michael Singer
    (spirituality)

Poetry

All Along You Were Blooming: Thoughts for Boundless Living by Morgan
    Harper Nichols (poetry collection)
Inward by Yung Pueblo (spirituality)

G

Grief

Grief comes with loss, whether that's through death, the end of a
relationship, the loss of part of our health, or any kind of significant
change, for example, moving house or losing a job. Life is a series
of losses and we all face some form of loss over time. A universal
experience, it's acutely painful and complex. *Grief is the Thing with
Feathers,* Max Porter's beautiful, short novel and meditation on grief,
captures this fleeting and transient experience, accurately examining the complexity of grief, and taking us on a journey of emotions
through denial, anger, bargaining, sadness and despair to acceptance.
Through novels, memoir and self-help, we understand and recognise
these emotions in ourselves, connect with others who've experienced
loss and learn to express our feelings, finding peace and relief.

Fiction

The Sky is Everywhere by Jandy Nelson (novel)
Grief is the Thing with Feathers by Max Porter (novel)
The Salt House by Lisa Duffy (novel)
Lily and the Octopus by Steven Rowley (novel)
What We Lose by Zinzi Clemmons (novel)
The Beginner's Goodbye by Anne Tyler (novel)

Non-fiction

The Year of Magical Thinking by Joan Didion (memoir)
A Grief Observed by C.S. Lewis (memoir)
It's OK That You're Not OK by Megan Devine (psychology, self-help)
In Love: A Memoir of Love and Loss by Amy Bloom (memoir)
Languages of Loss: A Psychotherapist's Journey Through Grief by Sasha
    Bates (memoir)
The Choice: Embrace the Possible by Dr Edith Eva Eger (memoir)
*The Grieving Brain: The Surprising Science of How We Learn from Love and
    Loss* by Mary-Frances O'Connor (psychology)
Option B by Sheryl Sandberg and Adam Grant (self-help)
Do Death: For a Life Better Lived by Amanda Blainey (self-help)
Breaking Sad by Shelly Fisher and Jennifer Jones (self-help)
*Healing the Adult Sibling's Grieving Heart: 100 Practical Ideas After Your
    Brother or Sister Dies* by Alan D. Wolfelt (self-help)
Grief Works: Stories of Life, Death and Surviving by Julia Samuel
    (psychology, self-help)
Last Things: A Graphic Memoir of Loss and Love by Marissa Moss
    (graphic memoir)

Poetry

Somehow by Helen Calcutt (poetry collection)

Guilt

We experience guilt when we feel like we've violated a moral or ethical code and engaged in wrongdoing. It's often accompanied by feelings of remorse, regret and self-blame. It can be a powerful motivator to make amends, seek forgiveness, or take steps to rectify these mistakes. Prolonged or excessive guilt can be harmful to one's mental health and well-being. The literature below serves as an excellent exploration of the emotion of guilt.

Fiction
Beloved by Toni Morrison (novel)

Non-fiction
Escaping Toxic Guilt: Five Proven Steps to Free Yourself from Guilt for Good! by Susan Carrell (personal development)
Let Go of the Guilt: Stop Beating Yourself Up and Take Back Your Joy by Valorie Burton (personal development)

H

Hopelessness

Hopelessness stems from feelings of powerlessness and a lack of agency in a situation, for example when we're faced with an overwhelming challenge or feel trapped and unable to escape a difficult situation. We experience intense helplessness, despair and sadness. It's important to seek support and find ways to regain control and agency in these situations. The literature suggested below can help us feel hopeful again, showing us strategies for feeling more empowered to exercise our own agency, no matter what situation we find ourselves in.

Fiction
Forgive Me, Leonard Peacock by Matthew Quick (novel)

Non-fiction
Reasons to Stay Alive by Matt Haig (psychology, memoir)
The Boy Who Harnessed the Wind: Creating Currents of Electricity and Hope by William Kamkwamba (memoir)
This Too Shall Pass: Stories of Change, Crises and Hopeful Beginnings by Julia Samuel (psychology)
Yes to Life in Spite of Everything by Viktor Frankl (personal development)
The Little Big Things by Henry Fraser (memoir)

I

Identity Crisis

An identity crisis can lead us to question our beliefs, values, goals and sense of purpose. This may trigger feelings of anxiety, insecurity and confusion. Identity crises are a normal and healthy part of personal development as they allow us to explore different aspects of ourselves and ultimately develop a clear sense of self. However, they can also be challenging and uncomfortable experiences that leave us in need of support and guidance. You might find the following books helpful in exploring your values, goals and purpose.

Fiction

Half of a Yellow Sun by Chimamanda Ngozi Adichie (novel)
The Late Mattia Pascal by Luigi Pirandello (novel)
No Longer Human by Osamu Dazai (novel)
White Teeth by Zadie Smith (novel)
Saltwater by Jessica Andrews (novel)

Non-fiction

The Lies That Bind: Re-thinking Identity by Kwame Anthony Appiah
        (philosophy, psychology)
Status Game by Will Storr (psychology, sociology)
Identity: A Very Short Introduction by Florian Coulmas (psychology,
        sociology)
On Identity by Amin Maalouf (psychology, philosophy)
Stranger in the Mirror: The Scientific Search for the Self by Robert Levine
        (philosophy)

Infertility

When we're faced with infertility issues, it's important to take care of ourselves emotionally and physically. We may need to process feelings of grief, anger and frustration. Engaging in self-care activities, such as reading, exercise or meditation, can help reduce the level of stress we experience and improve overall well-being. It's also important to remember that your fertility should not define your worth, and that there are many different paths to building a family. The following books may offer a path forward.

Fiction

Brood by Jackie Polzin (novel)
The Light Between Oceans by M. L. Stedman (novel)
Stay With Me by Ayọ̀bámi Adébáyọ̀ (novel)

Non-fiction

Notes to Self by Emilie Pine (essays – see essay titled 'From the Baby Years')
The Art of Waiting: On Fertility, Medicine, and Motherhood by Belle Boggs (memoir)
Silent Sorority: A Barren Woman Gets Busy, Angry, Lost and Found by Pamela Mahoney Tsigdinos (memoir)
It Starts with the Egg: How the Science of Egg Quality Can Help You Get Pregnant Naturally, Prevent Miscarriage, and Improve Your Odds in IVF by Rebecca Fett (health)

Insomnia

An extremely frustrating condition to deal with, insomnia plays havoc with our minds both during the day and at night, affecting our moods, productivity and overall quality of life. While we may need professional help to address our sleeplessness, we may also find comfort and support in the following literature, including a poetry collection on insomnia.

Fiction

After Dark by Haruki Murakami (novel)
Compass by Mathias Énard (novel)

Non-fiction

Nothing: A Portrait of Insomnia by Blake Butler (memoir)
Insomnia by Marina Benjamin (memoir)
Why We Sleep: Unlocking the Power of Sleep and Dreams by Matthew
    Walker (neuroscience)
Awakenings by Oliver Sacks (psychology, neuroscience)
Sleep Rituals: 100 Practices for a Deep and Peaceful Sleep by Jennifer
    Williamson (self-help)

Poetry

Acquainted with the Night: Insomnia Poems by Lisa Russ Spaar (poetry
    collection)

Intimacy

A lack of intimacy with our partners can bring on an acute sense of
disconnection, and even rejection and abandonment. It can affect our
self-esteem, as we may feel unattractive or undesired. We may also
feel loss or grief for the intimacy we once had, and we may long for
the closeness, affection and emotional support we used to share with
our partner. The following literature offers guidance for rebuilding
and restoring the intimacy we once had.

Fiction

Prepare Her by Genevieve Plunkett (short story collection)
Mr Fox by Helen Oyeyemi (novel)
Still Life by Sarah Winman (novel)
The Notebook by Nicholas Sparks (novel)
Olive Kitteridge by Elizabeth Strout (novel)
What Happens at Night by Peter Cameron (novel)

Non-fiction

Three Women by Lisa Taddeo (reportage)

Sex with Shakespeare by Jillian Keenan (memoir)

The 5 Love Languages: How to Express Heartfelt Commitment to Your Mate by Gary Chapman (personal development)

The Relationship Cure: A 5 Step Guide to Strengthening Your Marriage, Family, and Friendships by John Gottman and Joan DeClaire (personal development)

Attached: The New Science of Adult Attachment and How It Can Help You Find – and Keep – Love by Amir Levine and Rachel S. F. Heller (psychology)

Mating in Captivity: Unlocking Erotic Intelligence by Esther Perel (psychology)

The Evolution of Desire: Strategies of Human Mating by David M. Buss (psychology)

Poetry

Love by Night by S. K. Williams (poetry collection)

J

Jealousy

Jealousy can be both a positive and negative emotion. The positive consequences of jealousy prompt us to address issues in our relationships or enhance our self-awareness. When jealousy leads us to behave in harmful ways, such as checking a loved one's phone, keeping tabs on their social media accounts, making unfounded accusations or acting in overly possessive ways, it might be helpful to develop strategies for managing the emotions jealousy triggers. These strategies might include building trust and improving communication in our relationships. Here's a list that explores themes of jealousy.

Fiction
Othello by William Shakespeare (play)
Wuthering Heights by Emily Brontë (novel)
The Kreutzer Sonata by Leo Tolstoy (novel)
The Interestings by Meg Wolitzer (novel)
Break in Case of Emergency by Jessica Winter (novel)

Non-fiction
The Jealousy Cure: Learn to Trust, Overcome Possessiveness, and Save Your Relationship by Robert L. Leahy (personal development)
Jealousy by Marcel Proust (psychology)

K

Kainotophobia (Fear of Change)

Change is always hard because it involves facing loss – the loss of an activity, person or life that we were previously used to. The fear of change can manifest in various ways: avoiding new experiences or challenges, sticking to familiar patterns or habits, closing ourselves to new opportunities for growth and development, or feeling distressed when faced with an unexpected situation. When you're limited by your reluctance to embrace change, it can lead to a serious sense of dissatisfaction.

Fiction
Mrs Palfrey at the Claremont by Elizabeth Taylor (novel)
The Change by Kirsten Miller (novel)

Non-fiction
Educated by Tara Westover (memoir)
Tuesdays with Morrie by Mitch Albom (memoir)
Walden by Henry David Thoreau (memoir, philosophy)
Meditations by Marcus Aurelius (philosophy)
The Art of Possibility: Transforming Professional and Personal Life by
    Rosamund Stone Zander and Benjamin Zander (personal
    development)
*Emotional Agility: Get Unstuck, Embrace Change and Thrive in Work and
    Life* by Susan David (personal development)
*The Lightmaker's Manifesto: How to Work for Change Without Losing Your
    Joy* by Karen Walrond (personal development)
Taking the Leap: Freeing Ourselves from Old Habits and Fears by Pema
    Chödrön (personal development)

L

Leadership

Leadership involves continuous learning, personal development and
practice. It involves building self-awareness and effective interpersonal
skills, finding good mentors and coaches to support your journey, and
fostering a positive and empowered culture. The following literature
provides helpful insights on the leadership journey through fictional
storytelling and psychological and philosophical non-fiction.

Fiction
Things Fall Apart by Chinua Achebe (novel)
Julius Caesar by William Shakespeare (play)
Death of a Salesman by Arthur Miller (play)
Antigone by Sophocles (play)

Non-fiction
The Art of War by Sun Tzu (philosophy)
The Art of Gathering: How We Meet and Why it Matters by Priya Parker
    (psychology, sociology)
Dare to Lead: Brave Work. Tough Conversations. Whole Hearts by Brené
    Brown (psychology)
Originals: How Non-Conformists Move the World by Adam M. Grant
    (psychology)
Shoe Dog: A Memoir by the Creator of Nike by Phil Knight (memoir)

LGBQT+

LGBQT+ literature refers to written works that focus on, or feature, characters who identify as lesbian, gay, bisexual, transgender, queer or other non-heterosexual or cisgender identities. This type of literature represents and explores the diverse experiences of LGBQT+ people, including their struggles, triumphs, relationships and identities. LGBQT+ literature has played an important role in shaping public discourse around issues related to sexuality and gender identity. It's provided a platform for LGBQT+ writers to share their stories and experiences, and has raised awareness and understanding of the LGBQT+ community. Here's a diverse selection of LGBQT+ literature, including novels, memoirs, autobiographies, essay collections and poetry.

Fiction

The Price of Salt, or Carol by Patricia Highsmith (novel)
Notes of a Crocodile by Qiu Miaojin (novel)
Not One Day by Anne Garréta (novel)
After Delores by Sarah Schulman (novel)
The Great Believers by Rebecca Makkai (novel)
The Heart's Invisible Furies by John Boyne (novel)
Memorial by Bryan Washington (novel)
All of You Every Single One by Beatrice Hitchman (novel)
An Ordinary Wonder by Buki Papillon (novel)
Conversations with Friends by Sally Rooney (novel)
Box Hill by Adam Mars-Jones (novel)
Cleanness by Garth Greenwell (novel)
Exciting Times by Naoise Dolan (novel)
Less by Andrew Sean Greer (novel)

Non-fiction

My Autobiography of Carson McCullers by Jenn Shapland (memoir)
A Dutiful Boy: A Memoir of a Gay Muslim's Journey to Acceptance by
        Mohsin Zaidi (memoir)
A Visible Man by Edward Enninful (memoir)
Are You This? Or Are You This? A Story of Identity and Worth by Madian Al
        Jazerah and Ellen Georgiou (memoir)
Burning My Roti: Breaking Barriers as a Queer Indian Woman by Sharan
        Dhaliwal (memoir)
Why Be Happy When You Could Be Normal? by Jeanette
        Winterson (memoir)
All In by Billie Jean King (memoir)
Alan Turing: The Enigma by Andrew Hodges (biography)
How to be a Girl: A Mother's Memoir of Raising her Transgender Daughter
        by Marlo Mack (memoir)

In the Dream House by Carmen Maria Machado (memoir)
Lost and Found by Kathryn Schulz (memoir)
Love Letters: Vita and Virginia by Vita Sackville-West and Virginia
     Woolf (letters)
Spectrums: Autistic Transgender People in Their Own Words by Maxfield
     Sparrow (essay collection)
Strangers: Homosexual Love in the Nineteenth Century by Graham
     Robb (history)
The Magician by Colm Tóibín (biography)
Until I Meet My Husband by Ryousuke Nanasaki (essay collection)
*Wayward Lives, Beautiful Experiments: Intimate Histories of Riotous Black
     Girls, Troublesome Women and Queer Radicals* by Saidiya Hartman
     (history, feminism, sociology)
What It Feels Like for a Girl by Paris Lees (biography)
Wow, No Thank You by Samantha Irby (essay collection)
Fun Home: A Family Tragicomic by Alison Bechdel (graphic memoir)
My Lesbian Experience with Loneliness by Kabi Nagata (graphic memoir)

Poetry
Coming Home to Her: Poems about Love, Sexuality, and Being Human by
     Emily Juniper (poetry collection)

Loneliness

Loneliness, a universal human emotion, has been explored in literature for centuries. Many authors have written about loneliness, either
in works of fiction or by sharing their own personal experiences.
Here's a list of literature that helps us navigate loneliness.

Fiction
Men Without Women by Haruki Murakami (novel)
Convenience Store Woman by Sayaka Murata (novel)
All the Light We Cannot See by Anthony Doerr (novel)
Eleanor Oliphant Is Completely Fine by Gail Honeyman (novel)

Non-fiction
The Lonely City by Olivia Laing (memoir)
Platonic: How the Science of Attachment Can Help You Make – and Keep – Friends by Marisa Franco (psychology, relationships)
Solitude: In Pursuit of a Singular Life in a Crowded World by Michael Harris (psychology, philosophy)

Poetry
Eternal Echoes: Exploring Our Hunger to Belong by John O'Donohue (poetry collection)

M

Menopause

Menopause is a natural biological process that marks the end of a woman's reproductive years. It typically occurs between the ages of forty-five and fifty-five, but can happen earlier or later. A normal and natural process, it can have a significant impact on a woman's quality of life. Women experience numerous symptoms, including low mood, insomnia, hot flushes and night sweats. If you're a woman going through menopause or know someone who is, the following literature on menopause might be helpful. This includes novels that explore women protagonists' experiences of menopause, as well as memoirs, true stories and health books that provide a wealth of information on menopause.

Fiction

Mrs Dalloway by Virginia Woolf (novel)
Break of Day by Colette (novel, autofiction)
How Hard Can It Be? by Allison Pearson (novel)
Woman of a Certain Rage by Georgie Hall (novel)

Non-fiction

Confessions of a Menopausal Woman by Andrea McLean (memoir)
Flash Count Diary: Menopause and the Vindication of Natural Life by
    Darcey Steinke (memoir)
The M Word by Dr Philippa Kaye (health)
Menopausing: The Positive Roadmap to Your Second Spring by Davina
    McCall and Dr Naomi Potter (health)
The Menopause Monologues I and II by Harriet Powell (essay collection)
The Change: Women, Ageing and the Menopause by Germaine Greer
    (health, psychology)

Midlife

It is not uncommon to experience an identity crisis in your midlife that can result in psychological and emotional turmoil. If you're going through such a crisis, you might experience dissatisfaction with your current life situation, a desire for change or new experiences, and a sense of unease or anxiety about the future. If you're faced with a midlife crisis, you may relate to others' experiences in fiction or non-fiction. Here's a selection of literature portraying midlife stories that may resonate with your own experience.

Fiction

The Keeper of Stories by Sally Page (novel)
The Summer Before the Dark by Doris Lessing (novel)
Intimacy by Hanif Kureishi (novel)

Non-fiction

Lots of Candles, Plenty of Cake by Anna Quindlen (memoir)
The Middlepause by Marina Benjamin (memoir)
Midlife: A Philosophical Guide by Kieran Setiya (philosophy, personal development)
The Middle Passage: From Misery to Meaning in Midlife by James Hollis (philosophy, personal development)
Women Rowing North: Navigating Life's Currents and Flourishing as We Age by Mary Pipher (psychology, memoir)
How to Live: A Life of Montaigne in One Question and Twenty Attempts at an Answer by Sarah Bakewell (biography)
Hagitude: Reimagining the Second Half of Life by Sharon Blackie (feminism)

Mind–Body Connection

The mind–body connection refers to the intricate relationship between our thoughts, emotions, behaviours and physical health. Thoughts and feelings have a powerful impact on our physical health. For example, stress impacts our bodies through the release of cortisol. Chronic cortisol release impairs the immune system and contributes to cardiovascular disease. Stress also triggers symptoms of anxiety and depression, impacting our mental health. To understand the mind–body connection and the corresponding impact on our mental and physical health, the following books might be helpful.

Non-fiction

The Mind–Body Prescription: Healing the Body, Healing the Pain by John
    E. Sarno (psychology)

Molecules of Emotion: The Science Behind Mind–Body Medicine by
    Candace Pert (psychology, neuroscience)

Mindfulness and Meditation

Mindfulness and meditation have been studied extensively in the
fields of psychology and neuroscience. Both are powerful tools for
mental well-being and stress reduction. Here are some notable books
on the two.

Non-fiction

The Power of Now by Eckhart Tolle (personal development)

The Untethered Soul: The Journey Beyond Yourself by Michael A. Singer
    (personal development)

Wherever You Go, There You Are by Jon Kabat-Zinn (personal
    development)

Motherhood

From unexpected pregnancies, fertility struggles, postpartum
depression, uncertainty about motherhood and raising other people's
children to the challenges of being a single working parent, literature
today beautifully portrays the complex and multifaceted experience
of motherhood. These current trends in motherhood are reflected
in books that offer intimate and vulnerable accounts of these
experiences.

Fiction

That Kind of Mother by Rumaan Alam (novel)
The Joys of Motherhood by Buchi Emecheta (novel)
Breasts and Eggs by Mieko Kawakami (novel)
The Mothers by Brit Bennett (novel)
Little Fires Everywhere by Celeste Ng (novel)
The Push by Ashley Audrain (novel)

Non-fiction

Mothers: An Essay on Love and Cruelty by Jacqueline Rose (essay
    collection)
The Tao of Motherhood by Vimala McClure (parenting)
Of Woman Born: Motherhood as Experience and Institution by Adrienne
    Rich (feminism, parenting)
Motherhood by Sheila Heti (feminism)
The Motherhood Affidavits by Laura Jean Baker (memoir)
Black Milk: On Motherhood and Writing by Elif Shafak (memoir)
Things That Helped by Jessica Friedmann (essay collection)
An Excellent Choice: Panic and Joy on My Solo Path to Motherhood by
    Emma Brockes (memoir)
And Now We Have Everything: On Motherhood Before I Was Ready by
    Meaghan O'Connell (memoir)

N

Narcissism and Narcissistic Personality Disorder

If someone's struggling with an inflated sense of self-importance
and has an excessive need for admiration, they may struggle with

narcissism or narcissistic personality disorder (NPD). (Note that NPD is a complex and severe mental health condition that requires a professional diagnosis.) If you think this may apply to you or a loved one, it might be helpful to explore narcissism and NPD in more detail through the following fiction and non-fiction literature.

Fiction

The Picture of Dorian Gray by Oscar Wilde (novel)
American Psycho by Bret Easton Ellis (novel)
The Great Gatsby by F. Scott Fitzgerald (novel)
White Oleander by Janet Fitch (novel)

Non-fiction

Traumatic Narcissism and Recovery: Leaving the Prison of Shame and Fear by Daniel Shaw (psychology)
Malignant Self-Love by Sam Vaknin (psychology, personality disorders)
Rethinking Narcissism by Dr Craig Malkin (psychology, personality disorders)
Disarming the Narcissist by Wendy Behary (psychology, relationships)
Should I Stay or Should I Go? by Dr Ramani Durvasula (psychology, relationships)

O

Obsessive-Compulsive Disorder (OCD)

Persistent and intrusive thoughts (obsessions) and repetitive behaviours (compulsions) can significantly interfere with daily life. To understand these behaviours in ourselves, it's helpful to see them in others. Below is a selection of novels, memoirs and non-fiction works to help you identify and manage the complex symptoms of OCD.

Fiction
Turtles All the Way Down by John Green (novel)
History is All You Left Me by Adam Silvera (novel)
List of Ten by Halli Gomez (novel)

Non-fiction
Obsessed: A Memoir of My Life with OCD by Allison Britz (memoir)
Getting Over OCD: A 10-Step Workbook for Taking Back Your Life
    by Jonathan S. Abramowitz, PhD (workbook)
The Boy Who Couldn't Stop Washing: The Experience and Treatment of
    Obsessive-Compulsive Disorder by Judith L. Rapoport (psychology)
Rewind Replay Repeat: A Memoir of Obsessive-Compulsive Disorder by Jeff
    Bell (memoir)

Overthinking

Overthinking is often characterised by having the same thoughts repeatedly or engaging in 'worst-case scenario' thinking, expecting the worst to happen. It's detrimental to our health, so it's important to recognise when we're engaging in such behaviour and learn effective coping strategies to help us manage our thoughts and emotions.

Fiction
The Book of Laughter and Forgetting by Milan Kundera (short story
    collection)

Non-fiction

Be Here Now by Ram Dass (personal development)
Can't Stop Thinking: How to Let Go of Anxiety and Free Yourself from Obsessive Rumination by Nancy Colier (personal development)
Overcoming Unwanted Intrusive Thoughts: A CBT-Based Guide to Getting over Frightening, Obsessive, or Disturbing Thoughts by Sally M. Winston PsyD and Martin N. Seif PhD (psychology)
Stillness is the Key by Ryan Holiday (personal development)
How to Breathe by Ashley Neese (personal development)

Poetry

A Thousand Mornings by Mary Oliver (poetry collection)

P

Panic attacks

If you've ever experienced sudden and intense episodes of fear and physical symptoms such as rapid heartbeat, shortness of breath and sweating, it might have been a panic attack. The whole episode can be distressing and painful, but with the right tools, you can minimise their occurrence and impact. Here's a selection of books on understanding panic attacks and learning strategies to manage them.

Fiction

I Was Born for This by Alice Oseman (novel)
Symptoms of Being Human by Jeff Garvin (novel)

Non-fiction
When Panic Attacks by David Burns (psychology)
Panic: Origins, Insight and Treatment by Brooke Warner and Leonard
    Schmidt (psychology)

Parenting

Parenting can be a complex and challenging task. There's a vast
amount of literature available on the subject, with many subcategories
within this addressing everything from raising boys, sibling rivalry,
emotions and trauma to navigating children's mental health. Below
is a diverse selection of novels and non-fiction titles that address some
of the most common parenting challenges.

Fiction
Where We Belong by Emily Giffin (novel)
A Boy Made of Blocks by Keith Stuart (novel)
Little Earthquakes by Jennifer Weiner (novel)
Eleven Hours by Pamela Erens (novel)
All She Ever Wanted by Rosalind Noonan (novel)
The Crooked Branch by Jeanine Cummins (novel)
Everything I Never Told You by Celeste Ng (novel)
Far From the Tree by Robin Benway (novel)
Hamnet by Maggie O'Farrell (novel)
Boys Don't Cry by Fíona Scarlett (novel)
The Hand That First Held Mine by Maggie O'Farrell (novel)
The Lost Daughter by Elena Ferrante (novel)

Non-fiction
A Life's Work by Rachel Cusk (memoir)

*The Whole-Brain Child: 12 Revolutionary Strategies to Nurture Your Child's
Developing Mind* by Daniel J. Siegel and Tina Payne Bryson
(psychology)

How to Talk So Kids Will Listen & Listen So Kids Will Talk by Adele Faber
and Elaine Mazlish (psychology)

*The Book You Wish Your Parents Had Read (and Your Children Will be
Glad That You Did)* by Philippa Perry (psychology)

*Siblings Without Rivalry: How to Help Your Children Live Together So You
Can Live Too* by Adele Faber and Elaine Mazlish (psychology)

Between: A Guide for Parents of Eight- to Thirteen-Year-Olds by Sarah
Ockwell-Smith (parenting)

Raising Boys in the 21st Century by Steve Biddulph (psychology)

Hold on to Your Kids: Why Parents Need to Matter More Than Peers by
Gabor Maté and Gordon Neufeld (parenting, psychology)

*Adult Children of Emotionally Immature Parents: How to Heal from
Distant, Rejecting, or Self-Involved Parents* by Lindsay C. Gibson
(psychology)

Why Love Matters: How Affection Shapes a Baby's Brain by Sue Gerhardt
(psychology)

*Conversations That Matter: Talking with Children and Teenagers in Ways
That Help* by Margot Sunderland (psychology)

The 5 Love Languages of Children: The Secret to Loving Children Effectively
by Gary Chapman and Ross Campbell (parenting)

The 5 Love Languages of Teenagers: The Secret to Loving Teens Effectively by
Gary Chapman (parenting)

*The Highly Sensitive Child: Helping Our Children Thrive when the World
Overwhelms Them* by Elaine N. Aron (psychology)

*Parenting Children with ADHD: Successful Parenting Strategies to Handle
and Calm Down a Hyperactive Child* by Amber Perry (psychology,
parenting)

Never Let Go: How to Parent Your Child Through Mental Illness by
Suzanne Alderson (psychology)

Doing Life with Your Adult Children by Jim Burns (psychology)
Autism: How to Raise a Happy Autistic Child by Jessie Hewitson
    (psychology)
At Home with Dyslexia: A Parent's Guide to Supporting Your Child by
    Sascha Roos (parenting)
Parenting the New Teen in the Age of Anxiety by Dr John Duffy
    (psychology)

Poetry
Nobody Told Me: Poetry and Parenthood by Hollie McNish (poetry
    collection)

Pessimism

Having a negative or gloomy outlook, where we're unable to see the
bright side of life or notice opportunities that come our way, can leave
us hopeless and sceptical. With the right support and interventions,
we can develop a more positive outlook on life and improve our
overall mental well-being. The books suggested below can support
this process.

Fiction
Journey to the End of the Night by Louis-Ferdinand Céline (novel)
The Stranger by Albert Camus (novel)

Non-fiction
On the Heights of Despair by Emil M. Cioran (philosophy)
A Short History of Decay by Emil M. Cioran (philosophy)

Poetry
Canti by Giacomo Leopardi (poetry collection)

Positive Thinking

The phrase 'positive thinking' triggers mixed responses: a beneficial practice that promotes motivation and increased happiness, it can also masquerade as a form of denial and avoidance of negative issues. Overall, it's a useful tool for personal growth and development that can build resilience and increase well-being. The following novels and philosophy books strike the right balance between advocating for positive thinking and addressing the more distressing aspects of our lives.

Fiction
The Alchemist by Paulo Coelho (novel)
The Humans by Matt Haig (novel)

Non-fiction
How Proust Can Change Your Life by Alain de Botton (philosophy)
As a Man Thinketh by James Allen (philosophy)

Procrastination

To understand why we procrastinate, it's important to look at the underlying causes. Anything can lead to procrastination, including a fear of failure, a desire to get the perfect results, distractions, a lack of motivation and poor time-management skills. Understanding the cause makes it easier to step out of procrastination. The following non-fiction books help identify and address these causes.

Non-fiction
Deep Work: Rules for Focused Success in a Distracted World by Cal
  Newport (self-development)
Atomic Habits by James Clear (self-development)
Eat That Frog! by Brian Tracy (self-development)

R

Regret

The closed door, the road not taken, the missed opportunity – these things weigh heavily on our shoulders. However, we must remember that regret is a natural emotion, and to relieve it we must face it and feel it. Self-compassion, moral support and surrendering are ways of relieving ourselves of the regret we're dealing with. The following novels and self-help books highlight how other people have dealt with their regrets, allowing us to acknowledge and accept our own. Adopting positive strategies such as reframing, perspective-taking and letting go of the past by practising self-compassion can all help us move forward and face the future with positivity and a newfound enthusiasm.

Fiction
The Midnight Library by Matt Haig (novel)
The Remains of the Day by Kazuo Ishiguro (novel)
The Prince of Tides by Pat Conroy (novel)
The Post-Birthday World by Lionel Shriver (novel)

Non-fiction

The Power of Letting Go: How to Drop Everything That's Holding You Back by John Purkiss (self-help)

Better Decisions, Fewer Regrets: 5 Questions to Help You Determine Your Next Move by Andy Stanley (self-help)

The Power of Regret: How Looking Backward Moves Us Forward by Daniel H. Pink (self-help)

Resentment

If you've ever felt betrayed, unfairly treated, overlooked, or as if your expectations have not been met, it's natural to feel resentment. Reading about other people's resentment and anger has a calming effect on us, perhaps because we now feel understood, and as if our own anger and resentment has been acknowledged. Here's a list of some fiction and a self-help books to help you process feelings of resentment.

Fiction

Balzac and the Little Chinese Seamstress by Dai Sijie (novel)

The Yellow Wallpaper by Charlotte Perkins Gilman (novel)

Non-fiction

Birds of Passage by Denae Veselits (memoir)

The Forgiving Self: The Road from Resentment to Connection by Robert Karen (self-help)

The Gift of Forgiveness: Inspiring Stories from Those Who Have Overcome the Unforgivable (stories and interviews) by Katherine Schwarzenegger Pratt

Restlessness

Restlessness occurs for a variety of reasons. Sometimes it's the pressure to be productive, achieve more and set more goals. The following books help us find that elusive 'rest' state so that we're no longer compelled to constantly be doing something.

Fiction
My Year of Rest and Relaxation by Ottessa Moshfegh (novel)

Non-fiction
How to Do Nothing: Resisting the Attention Economy by Jenny Odell
        (self-help)
Wintering by Katherine May (memoir)

S

Secrets

There's a variety of reasons we keep secrets. Sometimes it's to protect ourselves or others from stigma. Other times it's to avoid being shamed or socially rejected. The burden of a secret can haunt us, leading to anxiety, stress, guilt or shame, negatively impacting our mental well-being. If you're keeping a secret and are unsure about disclosing it, the following novels and non-fiction might be enlightening.

Fiction
Secret Lives by Diane Chamberlain (novel)
The Vanishing Act of Esme Lennox by Maggie O' Farrell (novel)

Non-fiction
Inheritance: A Memoir of Genealogy, Paternity and Love by Dani
    Shapiro (memoir)
*The Secret Life of Secrets: How Our Inner Worlds Shape Well-Being,
    Relationships, and Who We Are* by Michael Slepian (psychology)

Self-esteem

Self-esteem issues are at the forefront of many mental health discussions and cultural conversations, yet many of us still struggle with low self-esteem, self-doubt and feelings of worthlessness. The good news is that we can develop a healthy sense of self-esteem – and here are a selection of stories and wisdom to help you do just this.

Fiction
The Keeper of Happy Endings by Barbara Davis (novel)
The Lucky List by Rachael Lippincott (novel)
Sparks Like Stars by Nadia Hashimi (novel)

Non-fiction
*What a Time to be Alone: The Slumflower's Guide to Why You are Already
    Enough* by Chidera Eggerue (self-help)
Healing Your Emotional Self by Beverley Engel (self-help)
*The Self-Love Experiment: 15 Principles for Becoming More Kind,
    Compassionate and Accepting of Yourself* by Shannon Kaiser
    (personal development)

The Gifts of Imperfection: Let Go of Who You Think You're Supposed to Be and Embrace Who You Are by Brené Brown (self-help)
The Four Agreements by Don Miguel Ruiz (personal development)
You are a Badass: How to Stop Doubting Your Greatness and Start Living an Awesome Life by Jen Sincero (self-help)
You Can Heal Your Life by Louise Hay (self-help)

Poetry
Self-Love Poetry: For Thinkers & Feelers by Melody Godfred (poetry collection)

Shame

When we feel we've done something wrong or something that's considered socially unacceptable, it's normal to feel shame. In fact, this can be quite healthy. However, when that shame becomes persistent, it leaves us feeling chronically inadequate, worthless and anxious, and at risk of social rejection. This type of toxic shame can lead to depression or low self-esteem. Here's a list to help you process shame.

Fiction
Shame by Salman Rushdie (novel)
Shame in the Blood by Tetsuo Miura (novel)

Non-fiction
Unbecoming by Eric Michaels (memoir)
I Thought it was Just Me: Women Reclaiming Power and Courage in a Culture of Shame by Brené Brown (self-help)
Healing the Shame that Binds You by John Bradshaw (psychology)
The Many Faces of Shame by Donald Nathanson (psychology)

Poetry
Days of Shame & Failure by Jennifer L. Knox (poetry collection)

T

Thanatophobia (Fear of Death)

Thanatophobia can be overwhelming, especially when we've come across death recently through the loss (or anticipated loss) of a loved one or a health scare. It can also simply involve intrusive thoughts that provoke an intense fear of death. These novels can help us explore our feelings around death, while the non-fiction books offer different perspectives on death, from the way cultures around the world mourn their dead to a psychotherapist's process on making peace with our mortality.

Fiction
Frankenstein by Mary Shelley (novel)
Memento Mori by Muriel Spark (novel)
Everyone in this Room Will Someday Be Dead by Emily Austin (novel)

Non-fiction
From Here to Eternity – Travelling the World to Find the Good Death by
      Caitlin Doughty (anthropology)
The Wisdom of Insecurity by Alan Watts (philosophy, psychology)
Staring at the Sun: Being at Peace with Your Own Mortality by Irvin Yalom
      (philosophy, psychology)
The Denial of Death by Ernest Becker (philosophy, psychology)

Dying by Cory Taylor (memoir)
The Tibetan Book of the Dead by Graham Coleman (philosophy)

Trauma

Trauma is a deeply human experience that elicits a strong emotional response. It can be linked to a deeply distressing event or experience, such as an accident, natural disaster, abuse or violence among others. Our sense of safety, well-being and ability to function is threatened, leading to a range of physical, emotional and psychological symptoms such as anxiety, post-traumatic stress disorder (PTSD), disassociation and flashbacks. Trauma has been captured extensively in literature through novels, memoirs, neuroscience and psychology books, self-help titles, and even poetry.

Fiction
A Little Life by Hanya Yanagihara (novel)
Beloved by Toni Morrison (novel)
The God of Small Things by Arundhati Roy (novel)
Eden by Andrea Klein (novel)
The Mountains Sing by Nguyễn Phan Quế Mai (novel)
PTSD by Guillaume Singelin (graphic novel)

Non-fiction
The Body Keeps the Score by Bessel van der Kolk (psychology)
The Many Faces of Shame by Donald Nathanson (psychology)
It Didn't Start with You: How Inherited Family Trauma Shapes Who We Are and How to End the Cycle by Mark Wolynn (psychology)
The Deepest Well: Healing the Long-Term Effects of Childhood Adversity by Nadine Burke Harris (psychology)

*My Grandmother's Hands: Racialized Trauma and the Pathway to
    Mending Our Hearts and Bodies* by Resmaa Menakem (psychology,
    sociology)
Maus by Art Spiegelman (graphic novel, biography)

Poetry
Bird of Winter by Alice Hiller (poetry collection)

U

Unemployment

If you're unemployed, you may experience a whole host of challenges,
including financial strain, loss of purpose or identity, and feelings of
isolation or inadequacy. It's important to remember that being unemployed is a temporary situation, and there are resources and support
available. The following books can help us to manage the emotional
toll of unemployment.

Fiction
The Forced Redundancy Film Club by Brian Finnegan (novel)
Temporary by Hilary Leichter (novel)
CivilWarLand in Bad Decline by George Saunders (short story collection
    and novella)

Non-fiction
The Sun is a Compass by Caroline Van Hemert (memoir)
*And Then I Got Fired: One Transqueer's Reflections on Grief, Unemployment
    & Inappropriate Jokes About Death* by J Mase III (memoir)

Why Losing Your Job Could be the Best Thing That Ever Happened to You: Five Simple Steps to Thrive after Redundancy by Eleanor Tweddell (self-help)

How to Find Fulfilling Work (The School of Life) by Roman Krznaric (self-help)

The Second Mountain: The Quest for a Moral Life by David Brooks (philosophy)

Your Creative Career by Anna Sabino (personal development)

The Obstacle is the Way by Ryan Holiday (personal development)

W

Wisdom

Wisdom here refers to the knowledge and intuition gained through life experience that allows us to navigate the challenges and complexities of life with clarity and purpose. It encompasses a range of qualities, such as self-awareness, emotional intelligence, compassion and resilience, and can be developed through personal growth, education and exposure to diverse perspectives. It often involves learning from our mistakes and failures, cultivating meaningful relationships, seeking out new experiences and engaging in self-reflection and introspection. Here's a diverse range of literature on life wisdom, encompassing ancient philosophical texts, novels, poetry, and modern philosophy and psychology books.

Fiction
The Celestine Prophecy by James Redfield (novel)
The Little Prince by Antoine de Saint-Exupéry (novella)

The Unbearable Lightness of Being by Milan Kundera (novel)
East of Eden by John Steinbeck (novel)
A Wizard of Earthsea by Ursula K. Le Guin (novel)
The Brothers Karamazov by Fyodor Dostoevsky (novel)
Siddhartha by Hermann Hesse (novel)

Non-fiction

The Beggar King and the Secret of Happiness by Joel Ben Izzy (memoir)
Man's Search for Meaning by Viktor Frankl (philosophy)
Love's Executioner & Other Tales of Psychotherapy by Irvin D. Yalom
    (psychology)
The Road Less Travelled by M. Scott Peck (psychology, philosophy)
Mythologies by Roland Barthes (essay collection)
*This is Water: Some Thoughts, Delivered on a Significant Occasion, about
    Living a Compassionate Life* by David Foster Wallace (philosophy)
Four Thousand Weeks: Time Management for Mortals by Oliver Burkeman
    (philosophy, personal development)
The Power of Myth by Joseph Campbell (philosophy, mythology)

Poetry

The Prophet (*Poetry Collection*) by Kahlil Gibran

X

Xenophobia

Xenophobia is the fear of people who are perceived to be different from oneself, particularly when it comes to nationality, ethnicity or cultural background. If you're experiencing xenophobia, it's important to recognise it's a learned behaviour. However, it can be unlearned. One way is to educate yourself about different cultures and ways of life, to appreciate the differences between people. The following books offer insight into diverse perspectives and experiences. Professional help can also be helpful towards identifying the underlying causes of your fear.

Fiction
The Constant Rabbit by Jasper Fforde (novel)
Animal Farm by George Orwell (novel)
A Very Large Expanse of Sea by Tahereh Mafi (novel)
Our Missing Hearts by Celeste Ng (novel)

Non-fiction
Caste: The Origins of Our Discontents by Isabel Wilkerson (sociology, history)
Wall Disease: The Psychological Toll of Living Up Against a Border by Jessica Wapner (psychology, politics)
The Leader's Guide to Unconscious Bias: How to Reframe Bias, Cultivate Connection, and Create High-Performing Teams by Pamela Fuller (leadership, social psychology)
The Origin of Others by Toni Morrison (social psychology)

Y

Yearning

All of us at some point have experienced yearning, a profound longing or desire for something that's absent or unattainable that can bring on feelings of emptiness, sadness or unfulfilment. This could be due to loss, separation or unrequited love. It could be a strong desire to be reunited with someone or something that's no longer there. Yearning can lead to restlessness, unease or even a preoccupation with the person or situation you're longing for. To explore your feelings of yearning, immerse yourself in the following stories of other protagonists who feel the same. You might be surprised at how deeply you resonate with them.

Fiction
The Time Traveler's Wife by Audrey Niffenegger (novel)
The Invisible Life of Addie LaRue by V. E. Schwab (novel)
Eleanor Oliphant is Completely Fine by Gail Honeyman (novel)
A Gentleman in Moscow by Amor Towles (novel)

Non-fiction
Bittersweet: How Sorrow and Longing Make Us Whole by Susan Cain
     (philosophy)

ACKNOWLEDGEMENTS

I want to begin by expressing my gratitude to my clients. Your willingness to collaborate, share your personal stories, and entrust me with your experiences during our sessions has not only enriched my professional journey, but has also contributed significantly to the development of my practice. I remain deeply indebted to you all.

To all the therapists who have touched my life, whether through brief interactions or longer engagements, your dedication has inspired me to delve into the realm of bibliotherapy and explore the profound impact that words can have on our well-being.

A special thanks to my literary agent, Kizzy Thomson, commissioning editor Bernadette Marron, and the team at Piatkus Books for giving me the opportunity to tell the world about the healing power of reading and for making this book a reality.

To my husband, Amit, for always believing in me and for your unwavering support and love. I am grateful for your thoughtful insights, ideas and patience, and for reading my words many times over. Your honesty and feedback have been instrumental in shaping my endeavours.

To my children, Arianna and Roshan, your enthusiasm, curiosity and encouragement have been a driving force during the creation of this book. Arianna, your little notes of affection placed on my desk infused me with energy and determination throughout the writing process. Roshan, your inquisitiveness and endless questions kept me going, page by page. I am incredibly fortunate to have you in my life.

To my parents, Kirti and Dilip, for instilling in me a love of reading. I can never thank you enough for the opportunities you have given me and the sacrifices you have made. Your support, kindness and unconditional love through the years, while asking nothing in return, has been instrumental on this journey.

To my parents-in-law, Urmi and Kantilal, and sister-in-law, Roma, thank you for your support and generosity, and for always being there whenever needed. Thank you for standing by me during this process. Your kindness has been invaluable to me.

I am grateful to my friends, Trushar, Artemis and Ching Ching – thank you for your support and believing in me. Your comments, praise and encouragement are deeply appreciated.

Finally, to readers everywhere, who have found solace, strength, and renewal within the pages of a book. Your dedication to the written word is a testament to the transformative power of reading. May your journey through literature continue to inspire and heal.

ABOUT THE AUTHOR

Bijal Shah is a bibliotherapist, counsellor and author. She is the founder of Book Therapy, which offers individual, couples and group bibliotherapy, literary curation and personalised reading services as well as bibliotherapy training. Bijal's book recommendations have featured in the *Guardian*, *Marie Claire*, *NBC News*, and various other publications. She's a member of the International Federation of Library Associations and the American Library Association, and has undertaken bibliotherapy workshops for the United Nations as well as various corporate organisations and libraries in the UK and the US. She is also the co-host of the podcast *Raising a Reader & Storyteller*.

Bijal has completed a post-graduate diploma in counselling and a post-graduate professional qualification in accountancy. She holds a BSc in mathematics from the University of Warwick and previously worked at Deutsche Bank and Barclays Capital.

She resides in Hampstead, London with her husband and two children.

NOTES

1. Freud, S. (1908). 'Creative writers and day-dreaming'. *The Standard Edition of the Complete Psychological Works of Sigmund Freud, Volume IX (1906–1908): Jensen's 'Gradiva' and Other Works*, 141–153.
2. Crocq, M. A., Crocq, L. (2000). 'From shell shock and war neurosis to post-traumatic stress disorder: a history of psychotraumatology'. *Dialogues in Clinical Neuroscience*, 2(1):47–55. Epizelus' story is believed to be one of the first recorded suggestions of PTSD in ancient civilisation. *See*: Hacker Hughes, J., Abdul-Hamid, W. K. (2014). 'Nothing new under the sun: post-traumatic stress disorders in the ancient world'. *Early Science and Medicine*, 19(6):549–57.
3. McCulliss, D. (2012). 'Bibliotherapy: Historical and research perspectives'. *Journal of Poetry Therapy*, 25(1), 23–38.
4. Green, K. (2020). *Rethinking Therapeutic Reading: Lessons from Seneca, Montaigne, Wordsworth and George Eliot*. Anthem Press.
5. Ross, W. D. (trans). (2009). *Aristotle's Nicomachean Ethics*. Oxford University Press.
6. de Montaigne, Michel. (1958). *The Complete Essays of Montaigne*. Translated by Donald M. Frame. Stanford University Press.
7. Rotenberg, C. (2023). 'George Eliot – Proto-Psychoanalyst'. *PSYART: A Hyperlink Journal for the Psychological Study of the Arts*.

8. Jones, E. (1953). *The Life and Work of Sigmund Freud*. Vol. 1. New York: Basic Books.

9. Freud, S. (1953). *Interpretation of Dreams*. Translated by James Strachey.

10. Freud, S. (1920). *Introductory Lectures on Psychoanalysis*. Translated by G. Stanley Hall.

11. Freud, S. (1908). 'Creative writers and day-dreaming'. *The Standard Edition of the Complete Psychological Works of Sigmund Freud, Volume IX (1906–1908): Jensen's 'Gradiva' and Other Works*, 141–153.

12. Levin, L., Gildea, R. (2013). 'Bibliotherapy: tracing the roots of a moral therapy movement in the United States from the early nineteenth century to the present'. *Journal of the Medical Library Association*, 101(2):89–91.

13. Brewster, E. (2007). 'Medicine for the Soul: Bibliotherapy and the Public Library'. Master's thesis, University of Sheffield, 75.

14. Galt, J. M. (1853). 'On the reading, recreation, and amusements of the insane'. *Journal of Psychological Medicine and Mental Pathology*, 6(24): 581–9.

15. Galt, J. M. (1846). *The Treatment of Insanity*. New York, NY: Harper & Brothers, 566; Galt, J. M. (1843). 'Report of the physician and superintendent of the Eastern Lunatic Asylum'. Williamsburg, VA: Eastern Lunatic Asylum, 26; Rush, B. (1830). *Medical Inquiries and Observations Upon the Diseases of the Mind*. Hard Press.

16. Jones, E. K. (1913). *A Thousand Books for the Hospital Library*. American Library Association.

17. American Library Association. (February 1939). 'A National Plan for Libraries as Revised and Adopted by the ALA Council, December 29, 1938'. *ALA Bulletin*, 33(2): 145.

18. Dufour, M. (2014). 'Reading for Health: Bibliotherapy and the Medicalized Humanities in the United States, 1930–1965'.

D. Phil dissertation, Virginia Polytechnic Institute and State University.

19. Gubert, B. K. (1993). 'Sadie Peterson Delaney: Pioneer Bibliotherapist'. *American Libraries*, 24(2): 124–130.

20. Shrodes C. (1960). 'Bibliotherapy: An Application of Psychoanalytic Theory'. *American Imago*, 17(3): 311–319.

21. Sabine, G., and Sabine, P. (1983). *Books That Made the Difference*. Hamden, CN: Library Professional Publications.

22. Djikic, M., *et al.* (2009). 'On Being Moved by Art: How Reading Fiction Transforms the Self'. *Creativity Research Journal*, 21(1): 24–9.

23. Shrodes, C. (1955). 'Bibliotherapy'. *The Reading Teacher*, 9(1): 24–29. See also: Shrodes, C. (1961). 'The Dynamics of Reading: Implications for Bibliotherapy'. *ETC: A Review of General Semantics*, 18(1):21–33.

24. Ibid. 18(1):25.

25. Kaufman, G., and Libby, L. (2012). 'Changing Beliefs and Behavior Through Experience-Taking'. *Journal of Personality and Social Psychology*, 103(1):1–19.

26. Djikic, M., Oatley, K., Zoeterman, S., and Peterson, J. B. (2009). 'Defenseless against art? Impact of reading fiction on emotion in avoidantly attached individuals'. *Journal of Research in Personality*, 43(1): 14–17.

27. Baikie, K., and Wilhelm, K. (2005). 'Emotional and physical health benefits of expressive writing'. *Advances in Psychiatric Treatment*, 11(5): 338–346.

28. Sawhney, N., *et al.* (2018). 'Audio-journaling for self-reflection and assessment among teens in participatory media programs'. *Proceedings of the 17th ACM Conference on Interaction Design and Children*.

29. Sherman, D. (2013). 'Self-Affirmation: Understanding the Effects'. *Social and Personality Psychology Compass* 7(11).

30. Fox, G., *et al.* (2015). 'Neural correlates of gratitude'. *Frontiers in Psychology Journal*, 6. Sec. Emotional Science.

31. Hazlett, L.I., Moieni, M., Irwin, M. R., Byrne Haltom, K. E., Jevtic, I., Meyer, M. L., Breen, E. C., Cole, S. W., Eisenberger, N. I. (2021). 'Exploring neural mechanisms of the health benefits of gratitude in women: A randomized controlled trial', *Brain, Behavior, and Immunity*, 95: 444–453.

32. Fox, G., *et al.* (2015). 'Neural correlates of gratitude'. *Frontiers in Psychology Journal*, 6. Sec. Emotional Science.

33. *Is The Man Who is Tall Happy?: An Animated Conversation with Noam Chomsky* (2013). Directed by Michel Gondry.

34. Zak P. J. (2015). 'Why inspiring stories make us react: the neuroscience of narrative'. *Cerebrum*, 2.

35. Schacter, D. L., Addis, D. R., and Buckner, R. L. (2008). 'Episodic simulation of future events: concepts, data, and applications'. *Annals of the New York Academy of Sciences*, 1124: 39–60.

36. Kleim, B., Graham, B., Fihosy, S., Stott, R., and Ehlers, A. (2014). 'Reduced Specificity in Episodic Future Thinking in Posttraumatic Stress Disorder'. *Clinical Psychological Science*, 2(2): 165–73.

37. Erten, M. N., and Brown, A. D. (2018). 'Memory Specificity Training for Depression and Posttraumatic Stress Disorder: A Promising Therapeutic Intervention'. *Frontiers in Psychology*, 9: 419.

38. Sumner, J. (2012). 'The mechanisms underlying overgeneral autobiographical memory: an evaluative review of evidence for the CaR-FA-X model'. *Clinical Psychology Review*, 32(1): 34–48.

39. Frith, C. D., and Frith, U. (2006). 'The neural basis of mentalizing'. *Neuron*, 50(4), 531–4; and Caracciolo, M. (2014). 'Beyond other minds: Fictional characters, mental simulation, and "unnatural" experiences'. *Journal of Narrative Theory*, 44(1), 29–53.

40. Kidd, D. C., and Castano, E. (2013). 'Reading literary fiction improves theory of mind'. *Science*, 342(6156): 377–80.

41. Berns, G. (2022). *The Self-Delusion: The New Neuroscience of How We Invent – and Reinvent – Our Identities.* Basic Books.

42. Berns, G., Blaine, K, Prietula, M. and Pye, B. 'Short- and Long-Term Effects of a Novel on Connectivity in the Brain'. *Brain Connectivity*, 2013; 3 (6): 590.

43. Sabin, R. (1996). *Comics, Comix & Graphic Novels.* Phaidon.

44. Green, M. and Myers, K. (2010). 'Graphic medicine: Use of comics in medical education and patient care'. *BMJ (Clinical research ed.)*, 340.

45. Hourani, L., *et al.* (2017). 'Graphic Novels: A New Stress Mitigation Tool for Military Training: Developing Content for Hard-to-Reach Audiences'. *Health Communication*, 32(5): 541–9; Carlton, N. (2018). 'Illustrating stories: Using graphic novels in art therapy research and practice'. *Psychology's New Design Science and the Reflective Practitioner*, eds S. Imholz and J. Sachter. Riverbend; Czerwiec, M. K., *et al.* (2015). *Graphic Medicine Manifesto.* Penn State University Press; Mulholland, M. (2004). 'Comics as Art Therapy'. *Art Therapy*, 21(1): 42–3.

46. Farthing, A. and Priego, E. (2016). '"Graphic Medicine" as a Mental Health Information Resource: Insights from Comics Producers'. *The Comics Grid: Journal of Comics Scholarship*, 6(1): 3.

47. Charon, R. (2005). 'Narrative Medicine: Attention, Representation, Affiliation'. *Narrative*, 13(3): 261–270.

48. Forsyth, M. (2013). *The Unknown Unknown: Bookshops and the Delight of Not Getting What You Wanted.* Icon Books Ltd.

49. McGurl, M. (2021). *Everything & Less: The Novel in the Age of Amazon.* Verso.

50. Klein, G., Calderwood, R. and Clinton-Cirocco, A. (2010). 'Rapid Decision Making on the Fire Ground: The Original

Study Plus a Postscript', *Journal of Cognitive Engineering and Decision Making*, 4(3): 186–209.

51. Dane, E., and Pratt M. G. (2000). 'Conceptualizing and measuring intuition: A review of recent trends'. *Academy of Management Annals*, 3(1): 1–38.

52. Lally, P., *et al.* (2009). 'How are habits formed: Modelling habit formation in the real world'. *European Journal of Social Psychology*, 40(6): 998–1009.

53. Lewis, D. (2009). Galaxy Stress Research. Mindlab International, Sussex University, UK.

54. Berthoud, E., and Elderkin, S. (2013). *The Novel Cure: An A-Z of Literary Remedies*. Edinburgh and London: Canongate Books.